SH*T
THE MOON SAID

A STORY OF SEX, DRUGS
AND AYAHUASCA

GERARD ARMOND POWELL

Foreword by
MARK VICTOR HANSEN

co-founder of the *Chicken Soup for the Soul*® Series

Health Communications, Inc.
Deerfield Beach, Florida

www.hcibooks.com

Library of Congress Cataloging-in-Publication Data
is available through the Library of Congress

© 2018 Gerard Armond Powell

ISBN-13: 978-07573-2086-6 (Paperback)
ISBN-10: 07573-2086-4 (Paperback)
ISBN-13: 978-07573-2096-5 (ePub)
ISBN-10: 07573-2096-1 (ePub)

Publisher: Health Communications, Inc.
3201 S.W. 15th Street
Deerfield Beach, FL 33442–8190

Cover design by Amir Magal of AMIRIMAGE
Interior design and formatting by Lawna Patterson Oldfield

I dedicate this book to my children, Patrick and Jerry,
who stood by my side and never gave up on me.

To my wife, Brandee, who walked the walk of change with me
and without whom this book would not be written.
She is my inspiration and my motivation.

To my loving mother Shirley, and to my beautiful sister
Claire, for always being my protectors.

To Michael Bernard Beckwith, Reverend Kathleen McNamara,
and Dr. Jeff McNairy, who all helped me find myself.

To Moughenda, a master medicine man and a lifesaver
to me, and to Taita Juanito and Mitra Poletti,
the other amazing healers in my life.

To the staff of Rythmia Life Advancement Center in the U.S.
and Costa Rica for their time, relentless dedication, and devotion
in bringing this work to the people of the world.

FOREWORD

by Mark Victor Hansen

Prepare to be amazed. That's what I say to people when I introduce them to Gerry Powell. I'll say the same thing to you as you begin to read Gerry's book. Prepare to be amazed . . .

What's so amazing about Gerry Powell? Let me explain. In my career, I've met lots of financially successful people. I've learned that being rich doesn't guarantee that someone is interesting, and certainly not amazing. Along those lines, F. Scott Fitzgerald once began a story with, "The rich are different from you and me." And Ernest Hemingway commented, "Yes, they've got more money." But Gerry Powell actually is unique—amazingly unique.

Although he never completed high school, Gerry became a millionaire while still in his twenties, and that was just the beginning. He "had it all," as the saying goes. That's impressive, but it's not necessarily all that unique, especially when you've met as many rich people as I have. When the "dot com" crash happened, Gerry suffered an extreme financial reversal. He lost his company. His net worth evaporated. He was deeply in debt. But in an amazingly short period of time, Gerry started another company and sold it at a huge profit. He was not only a rags-to-riches person, but a rags-to-riches-to-rags-and-back-to-riches guy.

Now this is getting closer to a genuinely unique story. It's certainly impressive from a business point of view. But is this why I consider Gerry Powell to be truly one in a million? Is this why I see him as one of the most amazing people I've ever met?

No, what's really amazing about Gerry is not his financial adventures. What's amazing is how Gerry suddenly discovered the key to transforming himself from a rich but deeply troubled person into an entirely different kind of human being. Not only that, but Gerry immediately made an astonishing decision. He would dedicate his life and his wealth to offering an opportunity for that same transformation to as many people as possible. Toward that end, he created the Rythmia Life Advancement Center, a state-of-the-art, luxury retreat in Costa Rica.

I've been there. Rythmia is the ideal environment for

inspiring revolutionary positive change. It's the optimal setting for rediscovering and connecting with your soul-self. Again, I've been there and I learned exactly what that connection means. Whether or not you visit Rythmia, this book will give you the tools you need for having the life you deserve and becoming the person you want to be.

As I said, I've met lots of wealthy people. I've also met lots of spiritual people. I've even met some people who are both spiritual and wealthy. But I've never met a person who is as committed as Gerry Powell to finding and living the truth—mentally, emotionally, and spiritually. Nor have I met a person who's devoted more of himself and his resources toward opening the truth to others. That truth resides in our own souls. We just need to connect with it.

This book is the story of what Gerry has done in his life—powerful but lighthearted at the same time—and it's also a guidebook for what you can do yourself. Prepare to be amazed!

CONTENTS

ACKNOWLEDGMENTS

Many have contributed to the creation of this book, and I am grateful to each of them for sharing their talents.

I am indebted to Mark Victor Hansen, who literally guided and coached me every step of the way.

Much love to my wife Brandee for directing and collaborating with Amir Magal, of AMIRIMAGE, to create the visually impactful book cover.

Much appreciation to Laura Alfano and Mitch Sisskind for their partnership in preparing the book content for publication.

And a special thank you to my publisher, Peter Vegso of HCI Books, who took on the final, important step of getting this on shelf, so readers like you no longer need to figure out the universal truths that will enable you to fulfill your life's purpose and find peace in your heart.

Part One

FINDING THE MIRACLE

Chapter One

THE PURSUIT OF HAPPINESS

This happened during my eighth or ninth plant medicine journey, when I was getting a real sense of freedom. I was "on the moon," both literally and figuratively. I was feeling so elated that I that told the moon I had a special request, and the moon typed, "What is it?"

I explained that this life had been so full of pain for me that I didn't think I could do it all again. So I asked the moon if in my next life she could make sure that I found the plant medicine as soon as possible, so I didn't have to go through everything again.

Her reply floored me. She typed, "Gerry, that's a request about next time, but it's the same one you used last time."

Does what you've just read make any sense to you? Plant medicine? The moon? The moon typing? It probably seems incomprehensible. In fact, I hope it does—because maybe it also seems intriguing. Maybe it catches your interest enough so that you'll read on. If you do read on, I can promise you two things. First, by the end of the book the paragraphs above will make perfect sense to you. Second, how you look at your life—and perhaps how you live your life—will never be the same.

ESSENTIAL QUESTIONS

Let's start with three essential questions:

1. WHY DOES THIS BOOK NEED TO BE WRITTEN?

That's an easy question. The Declaration of Independence, written in 1776, states that "the pursuit of happiness" is a fundamental human right. No other country has ever referenced happiness in its core documents. So let's go for it.

But if we're all pursuing happiness, as is our right, do we really know what happiness means? And what about *pursuit*? What exactly does that mean?

In the context of the Declaration of Independence, with its eighteenth-century language, *pursuit* means something more than *chase*. It's something beyond pursuing the baseball that's been hit over your head in the outfield or pursuing the best deal on a new car.

The Founding Fathers used pursuit to mean a continuing enterprise, as in a career or even a way of life. In this sense, you could say someone "pursued" a career in law or medicine. Pursuit, therefore, is quite a substantial word.

Now, what about *happiness*?

To the Founding Fathers, I doubt that happiness meant a night out on the town, a day at the beach, or another variation of an ecstatic or euphoric experience. I think it was more than that, and in the chapters that follow we'll be looking at what happiness really means. And equally important, what it does *not* mean.

One thing is certain. If we think of happiness as more than a trip to Disneyland, we may be pursuing happiness but most of us aren't catching up to it, let alone making it the centerpiece of our lives. Instead, we might be catching up to something very different. Unhappiness, the opposite of happiness, or the absence of happiness, is the daily experience of millions of people. I want to change that and I'm confident that I know how to do it. That's why this book needed to be written.

I do realize that putting an end to unhappiness is an ambitious goal. Can it really be achieved?

Sigmund Freud didn't think so. Freud, the founder of psychoanalysis and probably the all-time most influential investigator of human emotion, stated that the most he could offer was relief from phobias, obsessions, and other clear forms of neurotic behavior.

No, psychotherapy can't bring happiness, according to Freud. We have to settle for much less. Maybe we just have to be content with a lower level of misery.

> In his book *Studies in Hysteria*, Freud wrote: "Much will be gained if we succeed in transforming your hysterical misery into common unhappiness. With a mental life that has been restored to health, you will be better armed against that unhappiness."

This means that unhappiness is a permanent and incurable condition. We can make ourselves better able to deal with it, but we can't get rid of it. Happiness in a truly positive and fulfilling sense—which is something more than just the absence of unhappiness—is not even in the picture. Even today's huge arsenal of antidepressant drugs can't promise much more than what Freud offered over a hundred years ago. Those drugs, after all, are antidepressants. They combat misery. They can make you feel less bad, but they don't make you feel good. They don't offer happiness. They offer relief.

But again, the Declaration of Independence says we should look for something more than that. We should pursue happiness as a goal, and when we catch up with happiness we should make it the foundation of our lives.

Will we do that? I think we can. We should. We must. Happiness is our birthright. It's why we're here.

2. WHY THIS BOOK, WHY NOW?

Strange as it may seem, and despite the fantastic progress that's revolutionized the standard of living for millions of people, there is more unhappiness in America than ever before. Consider this: Compared to a hundred years ago, America has far less disease, less poverty, less racism, less illiteracy, less hunger, and less violence. There are still plenty of problems, but many of the most destructive issues have been diminished or wiped out. For example:

- In 1952 there were more than 50,000 cases of polio in the United States. The disease causes paralysis or death, especially in children, and the cause was unknown. Today, polio has been eliminated in America thanks to the polio vaccine.

- Between 1946 and 1963, the United States exploded eighteen nuclear bombs in the atmosphere. Several of these test explosions took place close to American soldiers and sailors, who later suffered abnormally high rates of cancer and other diseases. Thankfully, there has not been a nuclear explosion in the U.S. atmosphere in more than fifty years.

- In the early decades of the twentieth century, 30 percent of Americans had never attended school at any level, even for one day. One hundred years later, 88 percent of Americans over the age of twenty-five have completed high school and 31 percent have earned a four-year college degree or higher.

With all this progress—and there's a lot more, too—are Americans getting happier? No, they're not. Not even close.

The World Happiness Report, issued annually by the United Nations, surveys various countries according to citizens' perception of social support, freedom, generosity, honesty, health, income, and good government in their lives. These are important markers of happiness, and we'll have more to say about them in a later chapter. In 2007, the United States ranked third in the Happiness Report. But in 2016, America was nineteenth, a significant decline, behind Norway, Denmark, Iceland, Sweden, New Zealand, and many other nations (worldhappiness.report/ed/2017).

Freud may have seemed like a real killjoy when he described unhappiness as a permanent, incurable condition. But maybe his pessimism didn't go far enough. Maybe unhappiness is not only permanent, but rapidly getting worse.

Why is this happening? In his excellent book titled *Iron and Silk* (Random House, 1986), author Mark Salzman describes his experience of teaching English composition to a class of men and women in China. In an early meeting of the class, Salzman proposed a writing assignment: the students should describe their experiences during some of the traumatic events in Chinese history. There were many such events, including the so-called Cultural Revolution, as well as earthquakes, floods, and famines. But after making this assignment, Salzman sensed that something was wrong. The students were staring at him in disbelief. Finally, one of them said, "We have all seen terrible things in our lives. But why would we want to write about that? We should write about what made us happy, not what made us miserable."

Then Salzman realized that what he'd done was a uniquely modern American point of view. Even in the world's wealthiest country, we've become so acclimated to unhappiness that we often think it's the only truth. We think that if we aspire to happiness, let alone actually experience it, we're lying to ourselves or sugarcoating reality. We've turned unhappiness into a habit, or even an addiction. Breaking free of that is a big reason why this book needed to be written—now.

3. WHY AM I THE BEST PERSON TO WRITE THE BOOK?

You may be familiar with the phrase "poetic justice." It means "what goes around, comes around." Karma is another word for it. You reap what you sow. Do something ill-advised now, and you'll pay for it later. I experienced poetic justice for many years in my own life, but with a significant difference from the standard definition. In my case, the pleasure and the pain happened all at the same time—all at once, instead of one event after another. I wasn't punished later for what I was doing. I was punished while I was doing it. I was punished by the emptiness I felt, by the absence of happiness in my life despite my material success. And I did it all to myself. I was my own judge and jury.

Let me give you an idea of what that was like. I was living the American dream, a true rags-to-riches story. I was a high school dropout, but I had a natural ability to manifest great amounts of money. I became a millionaire in my twenties. I was married to a beautiful woman, had two sons, owned several homes, two planes, more than thirty cars, and I possessed riches that placed me in the top 1 percent. All my self-worth was based on creating and selling thriving companies. I had a deep need to be the best at everything and to have the best of everything.

But something was wrong. When I bought a new house, a plane, a car, a boat, or even a racehorse, two things always happened at the same time. There was the rush that comes with an extravagant purchase, and there was also disappointment—every single time. What was so disappointing? Sometimes wealthy people feel that no matter how much they have, it's not enough. They can't just have a lot of money, or a lot of the things money can buy. They need to have *all* the money, and *all* the things money can buy. That's impossible, of course, so they're unhappy. But my problem wasn't that I needed more stuff. What I really wanted and needed wasn't "stuff" at all, but I didn't know that yet. I wanted a new state of being, and instead I was getting new houses, cars, and planes.

My many addictions during those years—drugs, alcohol, sex—were certainly destructive to myself and damaging to the people around me. But if there was anything good about that behavior, it would be the fact that I was seeking a different state of consciousness. I was seeking it in all the wrong places, but at least I was a seeker. Eventually I did find out where to look, although it took a long time.

I want this book to save you all the time I wasted. True, there were some very exciting moments but they came at a high price, and not just financially. I can't just give you a magic formula, however. I need to paint the picture of my journey, and if I do it right you may find some insights of your own along the way.

Chapter Two

A HOUSE,
A PLANE,
A CAR, A BOAT

For the sake of its own survival, the human race has needed to continuously adjust. We've experienced an evolution of our physical bodies, but there's much more to it than that. Our evolution now needs to include not just what we look like or how we move. It needs to include the evolution of people's consciousness. This is my life's purpose. My goal is to advance the *evolution of consciousness*, with the understanding that this will happen one person at a time.

What does "evolution of consciousness" mean? It begins with understanding the true nature of thought. Or, more specifically, the nature of desire. Every thought starts with a desire. But the actions we take to fulfill our desires, and more importantly how we react when the desires are fulfilled or not fulfilled, express the current level of evolution in our consciousness.

To understand this better, let's look at how one of humanity's great spiritual traditions has understood the nature of desire. The word *karma* has become part of the English language in an informal way. Basically, it means that "What goes around, comes around," or, "You reap what you sow." That's simple enough. But classical Buddhist teachings go into more detail.

Karma, meaning *action*, is the first step in a three-step process that governs our lives to an amazing degree. For most people, this all takes place through the medium of material possessions and acquisitions.

THE NATURE OF DESIRE

Action: Suppose you take a certain action, like eating a piece of chocolate cake.

Memory: Because the chocolate tastes really good, eating the cake creates a positive memory.

Desire: The positive memory of the cake implants a desire for another piece. That desire may not be acted upon right away, but the desire has definitely been established.

Desires have the potential to become habits or even addictions:

Action: When you're feeling sad, drinking alcohol can make you feel better by temporarily relieving the depression and anxiety that are symptoms of emotional pain.

Memory: When the sad feelings return, you have a memory that this can be quickly relieved by alcohol.

Desire: When the first two steps have become deeply established, the desire to relieve the emotional pain through alcohol can become elevated into a need. The need can reach a level above and beyond anything else.

In the worst case, this karmic wheel can get bigger and bigger and spin faster and faster, regardless of the cost in relationships, money, jobs, health, shame, or anything else.

Even in much more moderate circumstances, there may seem to be no end in sight. But there is a way to get off the karmic wheel. It happens when:

1. We see who we've become, and the possibilities of what we can become by reconnecting with our soul;

2. When we reconnect with our soul/true essence to achieve that reconnection;

3. When we heal our hearts and take action based on the change.

I became a millionaire while still in my twenties. I built multiple companies from the ground up, companies valued in the hundreds of millions of dollars. In 1995, I started thatlook.com, the first company organized to provide mass-market access to cosmetic surgery procedures. Four years later, I took thatlook.com public and the company achieved a market value of approximately $150 million. Although this company eventually failed and I lost all my gains, it led to the formation of my next venture, called My Choice Medical. I sold that company for more than $89 million dollars. I had five houses, twenty-three cars, two planes, and even a race horse. I had achieved the American dream—and then some—but I also knew something was very wrong.

The more stuff I acquired, the more I suffered. I was drinking and taking drugs and often felt suicidal. Everything that was happening in my life—both personally and professionally—was pretty much out of control, or close to it.

When I sold my first company I celebrated by taking five women to a hotel where we all had sex. It wasn't really an unusual experience for me. Besides my wife, I was having sex with an average of about two different women a day. I would have them come to my office.

When my kids were in Catholic school and I was at the height of my craziness, I met a lady at the school whose kids were also enrolled there. She had been a featured model in one of the most popular men's magazines of that era. In a sense, she was a celebrity. I began an affair with her that continued for a couple of years. It didn't end well. Her husband and my wife caught us at a motel, which was a very intense experience. The worst part was, her husband committed suicide a few months later. I can't be sure to what extent, if any, I was responsible for that happening, but it was certainly one of the worst things I've been involved with. There were others as well.

My first business was a land development company called YRENT. There were offices in Pennsylvania to service the New York/New Jersey market, and I wanted to open an office in Virginia to service Washington, D.C. This was at the height of my drinking and drugs. I met a businessman whom I'll call Dennis, and we became partners in YRENT for Virginia, There was also a third partner, whom I'll call Frank. I would not describe either Dennis or Frank as the most ethical people in the world, and at that time I was not uncomfortable associating with people like that because I was one myself, maybe even worse than either of them. Perhaps not surprisingly, we eventually ran into a business dispute. Frank and I went after Dennis very aggressively. What we did was not illegal, but today I consider it ethically wrong. This made Dennis very angry.

Dennis asked Frank and me to come to Florida to talk things over. Like a scene from *The Sopranos*, we went out on Dennis's boat to discuss what was going wrong with the business. Fortunately, unlike a *Sopranos* episode, nothing weird happened while we were out on the high seas.

But that wasn't the end of it. About six months later I got a call at my office from the FBI. They wanted to question Frank and me about our connection with Dennis—he had just been arrested for murder. *The Sopranos'* touch was how the supposed murder had taken place on Dennis's boat, the same one that Frank and I had been on just a few days later. Dennis's motive had been another business dispute. Dennis was obviously a pretty hot-headed guy. Had the timing of our meeting been different, Frank and I might have been the ones who were murdered. I cherish both of these men now, as they are a piece of my story, an important part of my evolution.

LIVING ON THE EDGE, BUT . . .

I mention these experiences to give you an idea of what my life was like. It was a strange time. I was excited to be living this very edgy existence, but at the same time I was depressed by it. Sometimes I even felt bored by it, the way you can get bored with something that's stimulating at first but then just gets old and oppressive. One thing was certain. None of it was making me happy in any substantial way. Maybe like kids who feel a kind of giddy happiness when they ride a roller-coaster the first couple of times, but then they start to feel nauseated. That's what was happening to me.

Eventually I did discover where to look for happiness in the truest sense, but that discovery required a radical change in my basic value system.

When people start out in business, the goal is of course to make money. That's not only because of the things money can buy. Making money can be an end in itself; a self-reinforcing experience that's a way of expressing dominance over everybody who's making less money than you are. Of course, there will always be somebody who's making more money, but the point is to try to narrow that gap. I accomplished a lot of that, but it was surprisingly disappointing, which was something I never expected to find.

Of course, you might say you'd like to find that out for yourself. You might say you'd like to have a hundred million dollars, and if it doesn't make you happy you'll worry about that later.

With that in mind, let me clarify the message of this book. Let me be clear about what I'm trying to say, and also what I don't intend to say. I was not miserable because I made a lot of money. I would have been miserable whether I made a lot of money or not. I'm not against making money, and I'm not saying you should be against it.

What I am saying is that making money—or doing anything, really—is unfulfilling and even painful or dangerous if it's done with a fundamentally damaged and disconnected state of being.

Suppose you want to teach a small child how to swim. You might try something like this. Stand with the child at the edge of a swimming pool and say, "There are lots of invisible poisonous fish in the water, and if you don't swim across the pool really fast they'll catch you and poison you and eat you. So now I'm going to push you in the water and you'd better swim as fast as you possibly can."

Well, it might work. Some kids may actually start swimming when they hear that. Most won't, of course. Most will never want to go near the water as long as they live. But here's the key point. Even the ones who do swim will be stressed out about swimming, probably forever. That's because they were doing it out of fear. Even more importantly, if that fear was put into them by somebody who was a larger-than-life authority figure—in my case, it was my father—it may take many years and a lot of work before that fear goes away. In this book, I want to show you how you can do the things you want—whether swimming across the pool or making millions of dollars—without fear or guilt or stress or anger, or any of the other negative emotions that bring unhappiness to even so-called successful people.

From my own experience, I can assure you'll be a lot better off if you resolve your deep emotional and spiritual issues first, and that's what we're going to work on here. You may not want to take my word for it, although I hope you will. You may, like me, need to make huge amounts of money before you realize how little that can mean. I would not judge you for that, because after all I did it myself. But I promise you that one of two things will happen. Either you will sooner or later find a way to take the journey I took—the journey for which this book is the first step—or you will be destroyed as a human being by the emptiness you will feel. That's just the reality, plain and simple.

I've begun to tell you some of my story, but I'm not writing this as an autobiography. I want the stories you'll read here, whether they're about me or other people, to be a lens through which you come to see who you truly are and what you really need. You will see what you've lost, and there will probably be some pain from seeing that. But you'll also see that what you lost had to be lost, in order for you to find it again with overwhelming joy.

I can't give you a magic formula for doing that. I can't tell you that this book is like an Aladdin's lamp that will deliver your wishes just by turning the pages. But I can give you *Sh*t the Moon Said*. It's my irreverent way of highlighting the existence of our shared unconscious wisdom, the life-changing potential that resides there, and how you discover it in yourself.

I should say *re-discover* that wisdom, because it was there from the first breath you ever took. It was your destiny to lose touch with it, and it's also your destiny to find it again. This book can help you do that. Plant medicine helped me, but you don't really need the book or plant medicine to reconnect with your soul. There are lots of ways to do that. The most important thing right now is to recognize that the opportunity is there. I suggest you think of this as a journey, but not a journey to a distant place. The destination is inside rather than outside, so the only real distance is how far you've come from your authentic self. That may seem hard to understand at this point, but I'm going to show you exactly what it means. Onward!

Chapter Three

THE DARK SIDE

In the previous chapter I tried to paint a picture of my career, the emptiness I felt despite the professional success, and the feelings I had when I experienced a very profound transformation. What I did not describe was the dark side of my life while I was focused on making money and creating an over-the-top lifestyle. In this chapter, I'll look more closely at that dark side. Bad as it was, it eventually led me to the miracle that was the only way out.

I was not chosen for a miracle based on any special qualification or lineage. Maybe the most remarkable thing about my miracle was that it happened to me. If a miracle can happen to me, it can happen to anyone. And it does happen to anyone. I've seen that myself many times.

So I was not unique. I was not the long-lost descendant of an Egyptian pharaoh. I did not land here in a spaceship like baby Superman. I was born in Scranton, Pennsylvania, a very down-to-earth place, and that's putting it mildly. It was not at all like the planet Krypton. But maybe a little like Mars.

What may have been different about me were the extremes of my experience, the highs and the lows of it. Sometimes it was hard to know what to expect. Buying a new house or car could put me on a high, at least for a while, but the same purchase could put me into a deep pit of self-loathing. I've lived through a rags-to-riches story both materially and spiritually, but the rags-to-riches element was just a defining characteristic. It wasn't better or worse than any other miracle. Everyone's miracle is unique, and virtually everyone who visits me and my team in Costa Rica finds the miracle that is unique to them.

Since the age of thirteen, I was a high-functioning alcoholic. Despite drinking and other substance abuse, I could usually get through the day and even accomplish something. My life was wobbly but my businesses were super strong, like tall buildings with weak foundations. My life could take the businesses down, but you wouldn't know it from looking at them. The collapse eventually came in 2006, when I watched my father pass away. Up until that moment, my dad was the angriest and toughest man I knew. I always felt he was looking over my shoulder every moment of my life. He was never very pleased with what he saw. Pleasing him was my impossible dream, and it really was impossible.

Throughout his life, my father was a man who was not afraid of anything. He would fight an entire football team. But at the very end, my father was terrified of dying because of the judgment that he thought was waiting for him on the other side. As he lay dying in a hospital, I entered his room with a Catholic priest whom I'd known as a child, and who I had just by chance met in the hallway at the hospital. My father immediately spoke to the priest in a desperate voice.

"Father," he said, "can you save my soul?" Hearing my father, this very tough guy, speaking to the priest in such a helpless tone of voice was of course sad for me—and it was also frightening. I thought, *If he's so certain he's going to hell, what does that mean for somebody like me? It means I'm fucked.*

To watch my dad die slowly and in such fear made me question myself intensely. *We were so much alike in many ways, would we be alike in death, too? Was this what my death would look like?* I began to question the very foundation upon which I built my life. I had always been motivated by fear of my father and his disapproval. With him gone, the motivation disappeared but somehow the fear was still there. I began running scared. My more or less functional life began to unravel.

To escape my reality, I started injections of four to five sticks of Demerol, an opioid painkiller, plus drinking every day for more than two years. One day, my son came into my room and found me in a deep sleep, my arm bleeding from the Demerol needle still sticking out of it. For the longest time I believed that my son had seen this, but only lately have I discovered that he didn't. I'm so glad that I believed he saw me with a needle in my arm, because that was my second most important turning point.

That did get my attention, and I immediately scheduled an appointment at the most expensive rehab facility in the world. But when I boarded my jet for California the next morning, I derailed. I called an old girlfriend and we locked ourselves in a hotel for four days with enough morphine to kill us both. Finally, a close friend intervened. He literally threatened me at gunpoint until I agreed to enter the treatment facility. I was lost, alone, and desperate. My drug and alcohol dependency was worse than ever before. I was losing my family and I didn't know what to do. I was a multimillionaire, an alcoholic, a drug addict, and I had no idea how to get ahold of my life.

In the rehab facility I asked a doctor, "Can I get fixed?" To my surprise, his answer was clear: "*Yes*." The doctor kept a watchful eye on me throughout my stay and we formed a close bond. He provided the therapeutic, psychological insight necessary to help me discover the reasons why I was trying to cope by abusing substances. Since then, Jeff McNairy, Psy.D., M.P.H., has been my best friend, my personal savior, and now the Chief Medical Officer of Rythmia Life Advancement Center in Costa Rica, which is now both my life's work and my home. Around the same time I met Jeff, I was also introduced to the Agape International Spiritual Center in Culver City, California. For the first time, I was connected deeply with a sense of inner peace. I began meeting regularly with Reverend Michael Beckwith, Agape's founder and spiritual director, to bring spirituality into my recovery program.

After sixty days in treatment I was able to confront my demons. I saw that my destructive behavior was not only causing harm to myself, but was hurting everyone I cared for.

That's when I made a radical decision. After leaving the rehab facility, I offered to hire Dr. Jeff McNairy on a full-time basis, and with a significant salary increase. Jeff accepted this plan, and with his help some positive things started happening. I reconnected with my two boys, Jerry and Patrick. After a very difficult divorce, I moved to Malibu permanently and began connecting with more people in the spiritual community. But the battle wasn't over, and it really was a battle. For five years, as I fought feelings of profound inner sadness, I would inevitably turn back to alcohol. Once again, I began drinking to excess and dating numerous women.

My functional self was back. Anyone who met me at that time wouldn't think anything was wrong. By all appearances, I was on top of the world. A beautiful home in Malibu, more than enough money to retire, a seemingly fulfilling social life, two children who loved me, and I was always the life of the party. But it was all a façade. I was abusing alcohol and gradually spiraling out of control. Somehow I continued to maintain a spiritual life, but a disconnected one. Maybe compartmentalized is the right word. After being out all night, I'd look at my watch and say, "Oh, it's time to go to Agape. I better head over there." It became my routine. I'd get a dose of spiritual wisdom on the weekend and then on Wednesday I'd drive back over toward

Agape. But I'd pass a strip club and I'd go there instead. Then, when I finally left the strip club, I'd say to myself, *What happened? I had it all on Sunday and now I've lost it again. And it's only Wednesday!*

I was in touch with some of the best teachers in the world, and they were telling me things that were very true. I was listening to the extent I could. My mind could get it, but my physical self was still not feeling it. My brain was in tune, but my heart still wasn't.

This went on for five years. I was at one counselor or another almost every day of the week. I did some research and realized that the time I spent in counseling was equivalent to the hours it took to get a master's degree in business administration. I could have gotten an MBA but I was doing counseling instead. I didn't even get a diploma for that. I didn't know it at the time, but I was relying on money and charisma to hide the abused child I was on the inside. Deep-seated issues from my childhood were haunting me and preventing me from reaching anything like inner peace. In addition to desperately seeking approval from my father, I had been overprotective and nurturing toward my mother and sisters since I was a kid. Because nothing I did was ever good enough, my self-image was one of failure, emotional damage, and being unworthy of love.

Now, once again, I found myself alone, an addict and running out of options. I had been there before, and I felt like I had tried everything. I had put in so much time and spent so much money trying to fix myself, and I still couldn't see a way out of the darkness.

In the midst of my downward spiral, something came into my life that would change my course forever. It was completely unexpected, and completely outside the boundary of all the therapy and counseling I was receiving. Maybe it had to be that way. Maybe the only way I could really accept basic change was if I didn't think that was what was on the program at that moment. Anyway, I made a sharp turn that changed my life forever.

I had a girlfriend who was from the Philippines. For no particular reason, I said, "Let's go see your grandparents in the Philippines. We'll get out of here for a week." We were all set to go but then my girlfriend and I had a fight that resulted in her not going on the vacation with me. There was no reason to go there, but there was no reason *not* to go there. In the Manila airport I bought a ticket to the romantic island of Boracay and checked into a couples' resort. I was alone but, once again, what the hell. This was really the bottom of the barrel in a lot of ways. I was a drug addict, a sex addict, a wealthy man, and somehow I found myself alone in a couples' resort on an island in the Pacific.

What did I do? I put a post on Facebook about what a total mess I was and how I was ready to quit.

Incredibly enough, that post happened to be seen by a woman, who had been a friend of a friend, who had at one time gone through the same rehab program that I had done in California. I had been introduced to her there. She was now a shaman in Brooklyn. She wrote that she was going to be doing a seven-day silent retreat in the Philippine city of Cebu. She suggested that we meet, and we spent a few days together just on a friendship basis.

We got to know each other and for whatever reason she really cared about me. She also thought that I was salvageable.

One day she said, "Listen, Gerry, I had a friend who was just like you. He went to Costa Rica and did plant medicine, and when he came back he was a completely different guy."

I said, "Plant medicine? What's that about?"

"Oh, don't worry, Gerry," she said. "I don't expect you to do that. I know it would make you uncomfortable. But just for your information, I'll tell you a little about it."

She told me about a plant medicine that had a unique effect on many of the people who took it in a carefully conducted ceremony, with an experienced shaman and in a sacred space. The plant medicine brought on a psycho-spiritual journey, a kind of life review (think Scrooge from *A Christmas Carol*), that could be tremendously insightful, powerfully healing, and could literally reset the boundaries of who you are and what you're capable of.

Well, if the shaman from Brooklyn was concerned this might make me uncomfortable, she didn't realize how uncomfortable I already was.

I called my personal assistant, Haamid, and asked him to get my luggage together and immediately book me into the facility that the shaman had mentioned. We would meet at the airport. I wanted to leave for Costa Rica right away. I drank all the way on the flight back, but the plan worked perfectly. I got my suitcases at LAX and five hours later, when I got home, I traded my suitcases and shortly thereafter was at the Liberia airport.

At first glance, Costa Rica seemed like the Philippines in the sense that almost everybody was five feet, seven inches tall. But there was one person who caught my eye right away: a tall black man, at least six-three, eating a Big Mac with juice dripping on his shirt.

"Hey, Gerry!" he yelled. I figured this must be my driver. I walked over and shook his greasy hand. He introduced himself and said, "I'm your shaman!"

This was my shaman? Somehow I never imagined a shaman scarfing down a Big Mac. But we got in his car. He didn't drive like a serenely spiritual being either. He drove like we were being chased by the cops, cutting people off, weaving in and out, totally crazy. I had been drinking for days and flying all over the world. I was just trying to go with whatever happened. But when he said we'd be doing the medicine that same night I was definitely surprised.

"Tonight? But I'm not in really good shape. I may even be clinically dead."

"Well, we're doing it tonight, man."

My only thought was that I would need to get my head straight before we did the medicine. I said, "When we get there, will I have time to go in the pool?"

"The pool? What pool?'

"The one that's on the website."

He laughed. "That's the website, man!"

Apparently, I would be spending $2,000 per day on a place that advertised somebody else's swimming pool. Sure enough, when we arrived, the place was a complete garbage pit. You wouldn't want your dog to stay there. Dirty, everything broken, just plain filthy. I couldn't find a place to sit down because all the chairs were so dirty, so finally I sat down on the grass.

When I saw my room, it was like a tenement in some third-world country. The air conditioner was making strange buzzing noises. As much as I wanted to rest, I couldn't stay in there, so I went back out on the grass.

By now there were a few other people there, including Moughenda, the shaman. I said to him, "What time does everything start?"

He just shook his head. "Gerry, man, you need to loosen up. You're wound too tight. Loosen up a little, man." Then he added, "Your mind is all fucked up, too. But to answer your question, it starts at seven o'clock in the temple."

When seven o'clock came, I asked another spiritual seeker to take me to the temple. It turned out to be the garage. It was a three-car garage with no doors. Fortunately, there weren't a lot of old smelly tires laying around. The walls were covered with bamboo paneling.

Chapter Four

THE CEREMONY

The ceremony that accompanied the taking of this type of plant medicine began with a clear directive: write down ten questions that were important to me, and that I would want the plant medicine to answer. I wrote down my ten questions. There were already maybe a dozen people there, sitting or lying on little cots. We were told to sit in a circle on the floor, and the shaman stood in the center and talked for a while. I couldn't really follow what he said; maybe I was still drunk.

The next thing I knew, Moughenda was standing in front of me handing me the plant medicine. "Take it, man!" the shaman said. He sounded a little impatient, so I swallowed the medicine.

I was given a blindfold and told to lie down on one of the cots. The shaman said, "When you see something, raise your hand."

At that point I started to wonder how I ended up in Costa Rica with a blindfold on, wondering how I was going to see something. But then I did see something. It was a cat. I saw a housecat. But I didn't say anything. It really didn't seem worth mentioning. Couldn't I see something more exciting than a regular housecat? Well, a minute later my wish was answered. I saw a tiger, a pretty big one, a little scary. This was worth talking about.

I raised my hand and said, "I saw a tiger." It turned out I was the first one to say anything. A few seconds later I felt someone tapping a finger on my forehead. It was the shaman.

He said, "Gerry, man, when you see my finger, let me know." But I still had the blindfold on, so how could I see his finger? And it was a very thick blindfold. But then I did see his finger. I saw it very clearly.

Then I saw him standing above me and he held up three fingers. "How many fingers do you see?"

"Three."

"Good, man! Now look at the ceiling."

I looked at the ceiling, and then he said, "Make the ceiling disappear." I did it. I made the ceiling disappear and I could see the night sky filled with stars.

"You see those stars, man? Jump to one of them. Pick a star and jump to it. Don't think about what I'm saying. Just jump!"

It was hard not to think about it, but I did what he said. I picked a star and jumped. I felt myself flying upward, and when I looked back I could see my body lying there with the shaman standing beside it.

He said, "Fly faster, man!" He was very demanding. So I was going faster and faster. I felt the wind in my hair. Then I heard his voice again. "Look to your left! Do you see the moon? Go to the moon!" I did see the moon, and since I now seemed to be capable of anything I flew to the moon. It was easy! It wasn't a paper moon or a cartoon moon. It was the real moon. As I came closer and closer the moon got bigger and bigger. But then suddenly everything changed, and I saw a very different image. It was a computer screen with a cursor on one side, and on the other side was an image of the moon with my feet sticking out of it. It looked like I had crashed headfirst into the moon.

That had really happened. I wiggled my foot and watched myself on the screen in real time. I was in the moon! It was me I saw on the screen.

"Moughenda, what should I do?" I said.

"Say hello to Mrs. Moon."

"Hello, Mrs. Moon," and then a typed message appeared on the left side of the computer screen I was seeing. It said, "Hi, Gerry." I was pretty freaked out.

"Moughenda, what should I do now?"

"Ask her your first question." But I couldn't even remember my first question. Moughenda had to tell me what it was. Then I asked the moon the very direct question that was the first one on my list.

"Mrs. Moon, why am I such an asshole?" Here was the reply: "I can't tell you until you go get your soul." By the way, all this was recorded. Very often people are so disoriented by the experience that they don't remember what happened, but it's something you really don't want to forget.

Moughenda said in order to get my soul I should fly home right away.

"But which home?" I asked.

"The one you're in most of the time. The one you live in now." That would be Malibu, so I took off. Why not? I could do anything now. I flew up the coast of Central America, crossed Los Angeles, and landed on the deck of my house in Malibu.

That seemed perfectly reasonable now. It got a little harder to understand when I walked across the deck, looked in the window of my bedroom, and saw myself sitting in front of my computer.

I asked Moughenda, "What should I do now?"

"Go see him, man. Go see him and say that you need his help." Very well. I projected myself into the bedroom and said to myself, "Gerry, I need your help."

Yes, this was Gerry talking to Gerry. We were wearing the same clothes and were identical in every detail. But Gerry in Malibu wouldn't even look at Gerry from Costa Rica. Moughenda said, "Tap him on the shoulder." So I tapped him on the shoulder and said again, "Gerry, I need your help."

This time I got a reply, but it wasn't the one I wanted. He said, "I wouldn't help you if you were the last person on Earth. You're a liar. You break promises to me. Your word means nothing. And you're a drunk."

"What's he saying?" Moughenda asked.

"Um, he isn't going to help me."

Moughenda didn't like that at all. "Then I don't care what he's saying. Tell him this is your last chance. He has to help you."

So I told that to myself, or whoever it was that was sitting there. This time he said, "I'll help you under certain conditions. First, I'm your soul, and you can't separate from me any longer. You have to take me with you for the rest of your life. Second, whenever you plan to do something, whenever you make any kind of important decision, you have to let me know, and you have to do what I say. If there's any disagreement, I have the last word."

That seemed like a lot to ask. Maybe I could negotiate. "Is there any other way? Is there a Plan B?"

"No! There's nothing else. You have to agree or I'm not going to help you." I had no choice. I had to agree, and I shook his hand. Or I shook my own hand. It was a little creepy, but we had made a deal. Still holding my hand, he stood up and led me to the bedroom window. We were staring out at the ocean. But when I glanced over at him, he wasn't me anymore. Or he was me, but now he was me at three years old. He was me as a little boy. That's who was standing next to me now. Then he jumped off the deck and I followed. We flew from coast to coast. We wound up in Scranton, Pennsylvania, in a house that I hadn't seen in about forty-six years. But I knew that house. I was standing at the front door. It was winter, and there was a light dusting of snow.

Then the door opened, and I was inside my grandmother's

house, which I instantly recognized by the black-and-white harlequin floor. It was Christmas. I heard a Bing Crosby record playing. I could smell turkey and ham and the pine needles of a Christmas tree.

My whole extended family was in the kitchen, laughing and talking. They were alive, although in reality they hadn't been alive in thirty years. I could see them, but they couldn't see me.

The little boy walked me further into the house. We came to a broom closet. Even though nothing was said I knew I was supposed to open the closet door, which I did. Inside I saw my grandfather, who was completely drunk. I was there as one more version of myself, as a three-year-old child, and my grandfather was sexually molesting me.

"That never happened," I said out loud. Those were the first words out of my mouth.

Moughenda heard me. "What never happened?"

"I'm watching my grandfather molest me when I was three years old. But that never happened!"

He said, "Call your father."

My father had been dead for six years. Even in this bizarre environment of the medicine I was still aware of that. But I did as the shaman said. I called out to my father and my father appeared. There was definitely no small talk.

I showed him what was happening in the closet. "Dad, did that happen?"

He looked at me and said something that was just as shocking as what I'd seen. He said, "Yes, it did, and it happened to me, too. What makes you think you're so special?"

It was a life-changing moment, and it suddenly explained everything to me. It explained how I behaved toward women, why I had so many sexual partners without being able to feel close to anyone. Everything became clear to me in that one second.

This is how the medicine works. Time and place mean nothing. You can be more than two people at once or in multiple places at once. When I went back to the moon and asked the rest of my ten questions, I received beautiful, amazing answers—answers I could never have come up with in a hundred years.

I asked the moon, "What's the secret to life?"

She said, "Authenticity. That means stop shining a light on things that you're not." It was simple, clear, and straight at me.

We were all done and it was great. I knew things were going to go better. But I was still high on the medicine. I said, "Moughenda, what now?"

Shockingly, he told me, "Go visit your grandfather. Go right up to him and ask him if he's sorry." The next thing I knew I was in a hospital back in Scranton. I went to the seventh floor, room number 711. There was my grandfather, a lifelong smoker, hooked up to a breathing machine.

"Are you sorry?" I asked.

He looked right at me and said, "No. Fuck no."

But I asked again. "Really? You're not sorry?"

Finally, he started getting a little teary-eyed. In the end he said he was sorry. That made me feel so much better. *But what should I do now?* Once again I asked Moughenda.

The shaman said, "Now you forgive him."

This was a lot for me to take on so quickly. But I did it. I told my grandfather that I would forgive him, and it was really emotional. He cried so much, as did I.

Moughenda said, "That's very good. Now ask him what he's going to do for you."

But when I asked my grandfather, he said there was nothing he could do for me. Moughenda told me to go back to the moon. So I did. Now the moon had hands. They were cartoon hands, animation hands, and they came out of nowhere. It was a new feature.

Moughenda said, "Tell her what happened." As I told the story, some typing appeared on the computer screen that was somehow still there. The moon typed, "I know, Gerry. You don't have to tell me."

"But my life is really a mess," I said. "I need you to help me. I want you to do something important for me." Then things got *really* weird: I put both hands on my chest and opened it up, just like you would open a cabinet with two doors. I grabbed my heart and removed it from my chest. My heart was a soft, black stone, like a pumice stone. I put it in the hands of the moon, and she began to vigorously rub it with her hands, as if to remove the stained surface of my heart. She was cleansing it for me.

When she gave it back to me, I heard Moughenda say, "Put it back in your chest, man!" But as I started to put it back I saw that it had turned black again. Why did that happen? This was the first time in the whole experience that I was afraid. For one thing, I realized that I was *on* the moon, which might be a problem. Second, my heart—the only heart that I had—now seemed to be decayed, degraded, almost lifeless. Was this how everything would end? A fool goes to Costa Rica, takes plant medicine, and dies? I told Moughenda that I was worried.

He said, "Ask her to give you a new heart."

Well, okay. I spoke to the moon again. "Mrs. Moon, would you give me a new heart?"

Instantly, a beautiful new heart was presented to me. It was a perfect heart, bright red and beating. I took it from the moon's hand, put it in my chest, and flew back to Costa Rica. I could see my body lying there as I got closer and closer. I could see the top of Moughenda's head as he was beside me. Then I just rolled down and into myself, and I was back where I started.

Chapter Five

SEPARATION

I've tried to describe what I did, what I saw, and what I heard during my first plant medicine journey. But that's not all that happened. The most important part of the experience was what I felt. And the really important part of what I felt was the realization that *I was not the only one who felt that way*.

WE'RE ALL ON
THE SAME JOURNEY

I saw with perfect clarity that my experience was just one instance of a universal experience. Recognizing that fact was a life-changing moment for me. I saw everything in a completely new and much more insightful way. I knew that from then on, I would devote my life to helping as many people as possible to experience that same level of transformation.

In describing my experience, I introduced the idea that I had become separated from my soul, and the importance of restoring that connection. In this chapter we'll look more closely at what that means. This is extremely important, because that soul separation happens to everyone, with results that can last a lifetime. Everyone can also learn to restore their soul connection again, with lifelong results that are vastly better.

Let's backtrack for a moment. Let's go all the way back to the biblical story of Adam and Eve. As everyone knows, Adam and Eve were exiled from paradise in the Garden of Eden because they ate a piece of fruit from a forbidden tree. Many commentators on that story have wondered whether it was fair. Not only did God exile Adam and Eve from the Garden, but he also sentenced them to a very different life than they'd known in paradise. They were going to know pain and suffering. They were going to work, sweat, and even bleed.

But if God was angry enough to kick Adam and Eve out of paradise, why didn't he just destroy them? After all, God created them, so he could do whatever he wanted with them. Why didn't God just say, "The hell with it!"?

That's a valid question, and here's the answer: God kicked them out so they could "learn" their way back in. Why did they eat the forbidden fruit? Was it ignorance or greed? Or is greed just a version of ignorance? But how could they be anything other than ignorant when they'd never been anywhere except paradise? Didn't God understand this? But I think that's the whole point. They had to leave the Garden to understand what the Garden really was and what it meant. That understanding would not come easily, but God must have known it would come eventually. That's why he didn't just destroy his creations. God is a lot smarter than we sometimes give him credit for!

Biblical commentaries teach that Adam and Eve, or their descendants, will return to paradise, and this time they'll know where they are because they've been somewhere else. This time they'll know what they've got because they lost it. When we look at the Bible story in this way, it radically changes the conventional interpretation. Most importantly, it depicts the forbidden fruit and the punishment for doing so as painful, but not really a bad thing. Something good comes of it. It's something better than what was there before.

People separating from their souls in early childhood is a traumatic event. Between the time we're conceived and we reach the age of six, a split can happen. We separate from our soul and take on a new identity. We become someone else. That separation can be triggered in different ways. It happened to me when I was sexually molested. For a surprisingly large number of people it happens because they weren't fed on time. Others have had parents who fought, or there was alcoholism in the family. It can even happen while a child is still in the womb, if there's a loud argument or a violent incident. Yes, it's painful and it causes problems, often for many years. But it's got to happen. The shattering of your early self has got to happen so that you can put it together again, and you gain the power to do that by learning what you need to learn. Something you might think is a tragedy has an opportunity hidden within it, provided you have the strength and understanding to see that.

Does my saying this seem cold-hearted to you? When I tell people that a painful break has taken place deep in their past, virtually everyone can relate to that. If I ask people if there was a tragedy early in their lives, everyone can relate. Alcohol, drugs, domestic violence, car accidents, fatal illnesses, fires, floods, tornadoes, earthquakes: we've all had catastrophic experiences that seem to put us out into the cold. I don't intend to minimize any of that. But I ask you to look at it in a different way. Again, unfair or horrible or tragic as it may seem, those things always happen and they must happen.

The fundamental thing I learned from my first plant medicine journey was that I wasn't an anomaly. The separation occurs for everybody, and we're designed that way. That's what my father meant when he said, "What makes you think you're so special?" It's built into the experience of being alive. It's built into your human destiny. It's out of your hands. What is not out of your hands is how you respond. Not what you did yesterday, or twenty years ago, but what you do right now. The purpose of this book is to help you see the path that's right for you.

Originally, we separate to find safety. We think it's no longer safe to be who we were. We think we've got to escape, because we're not able to survive who we are. It's the feeling that we're not sufficient—that we're not enough. That becomes the default message of your whole life, and you need to keep reminding yourself of it because otherwise you feel vulnerable and unworthy. If something goes right, you will unconsciously find a way to make something else go wrong.

We develop a new set of priorities. Instead of wanting to love, we might want to be rich. Instead of wanting to be loved, we might want to dominate other people. Instead of wanting a sense of community, we might want power for ourselves. Instead of wanting to be joyful, we might want to be seductive or intimidating.

We create separations between people—who's smart and who's not smart, who's rich and who's not, who's good and who's bad—and the motive for all those separations come from the same source. It's our own separation from our soul, which is who we really are. This is what the moon calls "the keystone lie." All disease, all addictions, all sadness, all violence, all aggression, all hatred is the result of this separation, which is the keystone lie. At some deep level of our consciousness we always know that. That's why we try to distract ourselves in every possible way. Money and addictive behavior are two of the most common distractions, but there are many more. Use your imagination. The irony is, most people never even get the distractions they wanted. Most people who want $5 million never get $5 million. People who want the perfect high from drugs never get the perfect high. All they get is the distraction that comes from wanting that.

Even if they did get what they want, they would just

have to want more, or find some other distraction. It never really ends.

The amazing thing about the keystone lie is that it's gone in a second if you shine light on it, and it stays for a lifetime if you don't. The universe is constantly sending you messages about this. But you've got to reach the place where you're ready to see them. With my financially successful but emotionally disconnected life, I wasn't too different from many other people who are always going after bigger and better thrills and acquisitions—and missing the clues that were so important to see.

While this was going on, I certainly believed that I was the initiator of whatever was happening in my life. I was the one making it happen. But that wasn't correct. I was doing lots of big and exciting things, but I was doing them for reasons that I didn't really understand. The actual reasons came from the separation from my soul, although I was completely unaware of it at the time.

Some events in England during World War II provide a good window into the effects of soul separation. When the major cities of England were being bombed every night, a decision was made to move large numbers of children to safer areas of the country, even though this meant breaking up families for a significant amount of time.

A British psychiatrist named John Bowlby worked with small children who had become separated from their families. Bowlby developed valuable information on how this extreme emotional pain was processed, and it's closely related to the soul separation we've been discussing. In his groundbreaking "attachment theory" study, the doctor described some basic stages of how children deal with an extreme separation crisis. But it's not a simple progression. People often return to a previous stage, or go back and forth before finally moving forward. See if you recognize any of these stages in your own life.

STAGES OF SEPARATION

Shock and Numbness

Especially in a young person, the sudden pain of a crisis can cause both body and mind to function efficiently, or even to shut down in some respects. In a very short time a traumatic event can be pushed out of your awareness and into the black hole of unconscious memories. This can be a survival mechanism. The pain might be too much to bear with an everyday level of sensitivity and awareness.

Yearning and Searching

This includes wide-ranging emotions such as guilt and anger, yearning for simpler times, or wondering and worrying about the future. Sometimes there's a tendency to withdraw from other people, even family members, which may continue even for many years.

Disorientation and Disorganization

At first, the pain and loss can seem overwhelming, as if it were the only reality. The rest of life can seem unimportant or even unreal.

Reconnection and Resolution

This last stage can't really happen until a significant amount of time has passed. That means years—often many years. Unfortunately, for many people this never happens at all. The whole purpose of my work now in Costa Rica—and actually in everything I do—is to open people's eyes both to where they've been and to where they can go in their lives. It doesn't happen by itself, and it won't happen until you're ready. The irony of this is, most people are more ready than they think they are.

Suppose someone had come to me the day before I took my first plant medicine journey. Suppose they said, "Gerry, tell me one thing that's true and good about yourself and I'll give you a hundred thousand dollars." I would have said, "Yes, I'm a drunk, I'm a drug addict, but one good thing about me is that I'm a pretty honest guy." But the first really important thing that I learned from my soul was that I was a huge liar, especially when I said that I was a pretty honest guy. Because when I said that I was not only lying to other people, but mostly lying to myself.

However, once I admitted to myself that I was dishonest, I stopped being dishonest—because I told myself the truth for the first time.

> HOWEVER, ONCE I ADMITTED TO MYSELF THAT I WAS DISHONEST, I STOPPED BEING DISHONEST—BECAUSE I TOLD MYSELF THE TRUTH FOR THE FIRST TIME.

Somehow, when I did that, I automatically canceled the primary lie I had taken in at the moment of separation from my soul. That lie was the belief that *I am not enough*. That's the belief that causes us to separate from our soul, because we feel we're not enough, and it's dangerous for us to stay in a situation where we are fundamentally inadequate.

But once we stop living according to that lie, once we

stop lying and start being honest with ourselves, then at that moment we really *are* enough, even a lot more than just enough.

This is what the plant medicine tells you, or even shows you. If you ask the plant medicine, "Who am I right now? Who have I become?" the plant medicine shows you the answer to those questions so powerfully and so vividly that the questions are not just answered, but are eliminated once and for all. You don't wake up every morning worrying about whether the world is flat, do you? Do you worry about how ships sailing toward the horizon might fall off the edge of the world? You could worry about those things; maybe there are some people who do. But for most of us the question of whether the world is flat has been answered so convincingly that it doesn't even exist as a real question for us anymore. That's what happens to a lot of your questions once you're able to stop lying to yourself. The plant medicine has the power to do that.

Once you're able to let go of all your distracting questions, you will have an overwhelming intention to merge back with your soul at all costs. Sometimes people have a concern about the meaning of "at all costs." When I merge back with my soul, will I have to become a monk? Will I ever have sex again, or will I need to become celibate?

But reconnecting with your soul doesn't mean you become a saint and live on top of a mountain. It means the intentions of your life are different, which may or may not mean that your material circumstances change. It's just that whatever you have or whatever you desire aren't distractions anymore. You're no longer trying to fill up a hole at the center of your being by getting a new car. For the first time, a car is just a car, nothing more and nothing less.

Sometimes people worry that making this change will disrupt what's been positive and productive in their lives. They worry they'll be so blissed out that they won't be able to do anything else. Above and beyond material things, no one who has merged back with their soul has become a worse parent. No one has become a worse business owner or employee. No one has become a worse musician or athlete. The experience of soul connection multiplies. It doesn't divide.

MANY PATHS TO SOUL CONNECTION

When I say, "this experience," I mean the experience of merging with your soul. I don't mean merging with your soul through plant medicine, because there are many ways to do it.

There are an infinite number of ways, and that's something that has been understood by many of the great spiritual traditions. *Yoga*, for instance, is a Sanskrit word meaning union or connection, which immediately suggests the concept of reconnection that we've been discussing. The true intention of the poses of hatha yoga is not just to twist the body into strange positions. The purpose is to focus attention on the connection between the body and the breath—to show the union between those two realities that we usually overlook. In a similar way, karma yoga, sometimes called the path of unselfish actions, is the practice of recognizing connections in all events of daily life, and seeing those events as opportunities to bring those connections to positive manifestation. Everything is an opportunity for action based on spiritual awareness.

Kabbalah, the tradition of mystical Judaism, regards the loss of soul connection as an event that requires a process of healing (called *tikkun* in Hebrew) that needs to be undertaken individually by every human being, and also collectively by the entire human species. Like karma yoga, *tikkun olam* means healing the world in activities of everyday life. Of course, since we are in the world, when we heal the whole world, we heal ourselves as well.

My own path to reconnection was based on plant medicine. That's a path that many people have followed toward reconnecting with their soul. I want to emphasize again, however, that this worked for me, but it might not be everyone's choice. I certainly don't intend to "advertise" plant medicine, or even to recommend it. My intention is just to describe the tools for my life-changing experience and to state that those tools are available in an ideal setting for people who choose to use and explore them.

Whatever path you choose to reconnect to your soul, the essential element is what Jesus said: "Come to me as a child." Come as someone who has managed to recognize the distractions of modern life for what they are, and who wants to move away from them. It also means believing in the possibility of doing that; I'm living proof of that possibility. "Come to me as a child" means starting from the beginning, and always staying at the beginning, no matter how much time passes. What does a child think of a Ferrari? A child doesn't think of how people will envy you if you pull up at a restaurant in a Ferrari, or how much the Ferrari cost. Maybe a child would like the red color of a Ferrari, or the fun of riding on the highway with the top down, but that's as far as it goes. That's the beginner's mind, the mind of an innocent child. The beginner's mind doesn't happen by itself.

The human ego won't go down without a fight. Whenever you attempt something that involves fundamental change, there will always be moments of doubt that you must recognize for what they are: they're your ego fighting for its dominance over your life.

If you try to run a marathon for the first time, there is a signature moment that will occur no matter how long and how hard you've trained. A full marathon is slightly more than twenty-six miles. When you've run ten miles, or even twelve, you will suddenly get the feeling that you've made a huge mistake. You've been running for a long time and you're not even halfway there. Maybe you're being passed by lots of other runners. Maybe some of them are old enough to be your grandparents. How humiliating. You think to yourself, *What was I thinking when I decided to do this? Why don't I just stop and have a cold beer? That would make a lot more sense.*

This is your ego talking. It's your ego resisting the change that you're trying to impose on it. Something similar to this can happen with plant medicine. In the first few hours of the experience, you might find yourself disoriented or even panicked. You may think, for instance, that you did something in the past for a certain reason, but that's not the *real* reason. The plant medicine, or yoga, or meditation, will

show you the truth, but your ego may cause you to misin-
terpret or even ignore it. Your soul wants you to connect,
but your ego can still try to get in the way.

Chapter Six

INTEGRATION

There's a reason you're holding this book in your hands right now. There's a purpose behind your reading these words. I don't want to seem overly mystical, but I'm tempted to say you've been called by your destiny to pick up this book. Let's just say there's a reason. It's up to you to understand exactly what that reason is. That's part of the work you need to do for yourself. I can't do it for you, which is a good thing. Because when you do it for yourself, the reward you get will be something that you've fully earned. As you do this work of reconnecting or integrating your soul self, there will be days that I like to call "days of ups and downs." You may feel like a tremendous revelation is happening for you, like you're seeing the Pacific Ocean or the stars in the sky for the first time. That's a kind of euphoria, an intense and crazy high. And then a little while later you may feel like you're getting nowhere, and that all this talk is just a waste of time.

Those contradictory feelings can happen in quick succession, sometimes in the same hour or certainly in the same day. But the key thing you need to learn is how all of that is part of the same process, and that whatever you're feeling is exactly what you're supposed to be feeling based on where your consciousness is right now. Don't take any of those up-and-down feelings at face value. Don't judge the process of finding your miracle based on those feelings. That's a key message you need to understand.

Even if this is an unusually up-and-down day, even if you're feeling really high or really low at this moment, try to identify exactly what is causing you to pick up this book and read these words right now. What is the problem you need to solve? What is the issue you're working on? Try to be as specific as possible about it. Maybe there's a conflict in an important relationship. Maybe there's something going on in your career. What are you supposed to do? Those things can be very important, and I don't mean to minimize their importance, but for the moment let's call them "the little questions." How are they little? They're little because if you really engage with them, you'll start to get a very big answer. The big answer will dwarf the little questions, and the answer is always *love*.

That may seem like an overly simple answer right now. It may even seem like a cliché. But when you start to experience it by focusing very intently on the concerns in your life, you'll see what it really means.

When you see the beauty of that, you'll see how much bigger the answer is compared to the question you're asking. When you see the love that's the essence of the system you're in, you'll know that it's much bigger than "Should I look for a new apartment?" or "Should I ask for a raise?" When you see where you are in the larger system, you'll know what your true intention is for reading this right now, even if you think you're reading it with the intention of answering some specific "little" question.

The big answer to any little question is always love. I've also said that "love" can seem like an excessively simple answer. It's interesting, therefore, that the simple answer can at first appear in an amazingly complex form. For instance, I had a vision of an extremely complex mathematical equation. The equation consisted not only of numbers, but of all sorts of three-dimensional objects and locations and memories and hopes and fears. It was the house where I lived as a child multiplied by the number of minutes in a day divided by the first time I watched a baseball game. Somehow this mathematical equation included all those things, and the equation expressed the true meaning of all the people, places, and events that had ever been in my life, as well as the true meaning of the universe. The moon called this equation, "Mrs. Moon's math magic." Her exact words.

That was the sight that I had to see in order to realize my own intention. This can be frustrating, because we ask to see the intention behind who we've become and who we are, but instead we get taken back to who we were many years ago or something we did in the distant past. We want to see one thing, but it seems like the universe insists on showing us something else. I want to be very clear about why that happens. Sometimes, in order to see something, you need to look away from it. That happens if you try to look at a certain star in the sky. If you try to look at it directly, if you really stare at it as hard as you can, you won't be able to see it. But if you look a little bit off to the side, then you're able to see the star. That's a basic principle of human sight.

In the same way, when your attention is directed toward something like that mathematical equation, you may feel like you're being distracted. But that seeming distraction is really what allows the natural process of inner recognition to take place without a conscious, forced effort. In fact, that unforced natural process is the only way you really can see who it is that you've become.

Just asking to see your intention is so powerful that any kind of conscious work you want to put into that is completely redundant. Once you ask, the natural process of revelation is already put into operation. It has its own energy and it works by itself. As soon as you ask, it has already happened. You may not see the result at that same instant, but you will see it very soon. Once you do see it, even if you do nothing further in your spiritual development, your life will be totally changed. You will never be the same again. You won't think the same, feel the same, or act the same. That's the power that this recognition will have for you. That's what it means to merge back with your soul.

BEFORE AND AFTER

Before that happened to me, I was a not a nice person. In fact, I was a terrible person. And then the next day I was a completely different guy. That was manifested very clearly. Anybody could see it. If you watched a video of me three weeks before, and then watched another video three weeks after, you'd think, *There's no way it's the same guy!* That's how pronounced the change was. This is because I made a soul agreement when I asked my soul to merge back with me at all costs. That agreement can't be broken. It's like making a deal with the devil, except the agreement is with a very different kind of energy. You can't undo reconnecting with your soul. Once you've rung that bell, you can't un-ring it. You see, you split from your original self and you became another person. That other person was occupying your being. That other person is the one who grows up and becomes a doctor or a lawyer or an airline pilot.

That other person, however, possessed an inner spiritual identity—a heart—and that heart got beaten down. It was beaten down by the fact that it separated from its soul. That was the first injury. Thousands more followed. By the time you're in your twenties, your heart has absorbed thousands of blows, and that happens at all levels of your being at the same time. The moon said that your physical heart and your spiritual heart are inseparable, one and the same.

The irony is, the process of separating from your soul may have initially been seen as a flight to safety. Yet your soul is absolutely safe. Your soul has never been hurt, harmed, or endangered. That's why reconnecting with your soul is such a reassuring experience. It's a part of you that is totally safe.

In my process of reconnecting, three things happened. My soul came to me and showed me what a terrible, destructive person I had become. Then I saw that I could reconnect with my soul, provided there would be a binding agreement that the reconnection would be forever. Lastly, I saw that the moon would give me a new heart. My heart was so damaged that it wasn't just useless. It was a toxic and corrosive presence in my life. It couldn't be repaired. It had to be replaced.

This is the process you need to experience. And if you've read this far, you may have already begun that. You may already feel a new heart beating inside you. If you have not yet received your new heart, you may still feel energized and exhilarated. You may feel a new energy that inspires you to engage with the world. But you're not ready to love again. To do that you need to receive a new heart, because the one you have has been so fundamentally damaged. Once you have your new heart, you literally love everything. It's an amazing feeling and it can be disorienting. For one thing, all the people around you suddenly see you as a completely different person, and you of course notice that. And you love them. In the past you thought that love was something that you received from the outside. It was something that you took in, that you acquired. But now you see that love is something that you give. It's not a transaction. It's a gift. You are the giver, and the paradox is that this giving fulfills you rather than diminishing you in any way. Everything you've ever wanted is here for you, and it doesn't come from being loved. It comes from the act of loving. It comes from being so fulfilled by love that the fulfillment is constantly overflowing to others. That's what happens when a new heart is beating within you. But if that hasn't happened yet, if there's still any residual damage from all the hits you've taken, you're not quite ready yet to be overflowing with love.

When you are ready, it's really a lot of fun. It's like being in some alternate universe where the everyday laws of supply and demand and two plus two equals four no longer apply. You are a giver, but your resources are not lessened by the act of giving. In fact, the more love you give, the more you have. It's an amazing feeling! Your ultimate gift will be helping someone else experience what you're experiencing. To see that happen is the ultimate fulfillment, because it really erases the separation between you and another person.

You know that he or she is feeling what you're feeling, so you're together at the deepest possible level. The world is yours and everything that's in it is yours, but at the same time it's "ours."

We've said that once you reconnect with your true self, that connection is permanent. Once you've received a new heart, you've received it forever. But you may think you've received it before you actually have.

There were years when I used to attend Reverend Michael Beckwith's inspiring services at the Agape International Spiritual Center. Sometimes I would feel a very powerful effect.

I would say to myself, *Now I really get it. I'm a changed man.* That would be on a Sunday. But by Wednesday or Thursday I'd be living the same kind of degenerated life as before.

It was really confusing. I couldn't understand how this happened to me. It was like Doctor Jekyll and Mister Hyde. Here's how I learned to deal with that. During my first trip to Costa Rica, after taking the plant medicine for the first time, I was really walking on air. Once again, I was saying to myself, *I finally got it. Now I've really got it.*

I was literally in tears. I was sending e-mails to every person I could think of, trying to tell them about this miraculous transformation. I was apologizing to everyone for being such a terrible person all my life. I was getting ready to go home from Costa Rica, and Moughenda was driving me to the airport. On the way we passed a McDonald's, and since there hadn't been much food for the past five days we stopped to get something to eat. While we were eating I said to Moughenda, "Is there anything I've missed? Is there anything else I should know before I leave?"

Moughenda just looked me in the eye and said, "No, Gerry, you'll be all right." For some reason I was a little skeptical, like I must be missing something here. It felt like something was being left out. But I felt great, better than ever before, so how could anything go wrong?

I was dropped off at the airport, and that flight was the first time I didn't drink on a plane in at least thirty years. When I got home my kids were looking out the window and saw me arrive. They knew right away that I was different.

One of the first things I did was apologize to my sons for what I'd been like. I very clearly saw the pain I'd caused them, and also the terrible pain I'd caused my ex-wife. No one should have to go through what she did. That was a real moment of transition for me. It was very emotional. I was crying and my two boys were crying. How it turned out was not what I would have expected. I anticipated that they would start to show some of the anger against me that must have built up over the years. But nothing like that came out. It was the direct opposite. They actually started offering explanations for the kind of person I'd been: "It's okay, Dad, look at how you were raised . . ."

It was the same way when I talked with my girlfriend at the time. She meant well. Her intentions were very good, but she started making excuses for me. That's what I had always done for myself—that's what most people do—and now she was doing it for me. It was definitely an unexpected consequence of the change I'd been through.

The same thing happened with everybody I met during the next few days. Everybody saw that I was different, but there was one big difference that they didn't see. I was taking all the responsibility for what I had done. There were no extenuating circumstances anymore. Whatever I had done, I felt very deeply that I had done it all by myself. Everyone naturally assumed that I was in pain when I apologized for what I'd been like. They felt intense sympathy for me. Because I had changed vibrationally, they didn't want to see me in pain, so they tried to give me a way out.

But another part of my change was not needing a way out anymore. Saying I was sorry for what I'd done wasn't painful; it was an expression of love, and that kind of love is never painful. I found that everybody really wanted to help me. Even though I didn't need help, they assumed I did because I must have been so hurt at some point in the past. Their hearts were in the right place. I knew they weren't faking it.

This was true even when there was a long history of misunderstanding or not getting along. I'd always had a fairly tense relationship with my mother. We didn't openly fight, but there was a kind of "cold war" where she would say something vaguely hostile and I would respond the same way. But even that style of communication was changed, and it was because my whole vibration as a person had changed. This all happened in the first three days of my return from Costa Rica.

On the fourth day something very disturbing happened. I suddenly went into a complete panic. Why? Because I was beginning to realize that this change was going to be permanent. For the first three days it was a kind of high. It was a euphoria, almost an ecstasy, like being on a different planet.

I called Moughenda and said, "What the hell did you do to me?"

He said, "Don't worry, man, you'll be fine," and he hung up on me. I tried to call back and he wouldn't answer. There wasn't much I could do. Moughenda was in Costa Rica and I was in California.

That's when I reverted to my normal lifestyle for a bit. I went out and got drunk, did some drugs, and slept with a woman I didn't really know. That's what I would typically do when I wasn't feeling good about things. In the past, after I had a night like that, I would wake up the next morning and feel terrible. But this time it was different. I didn't feel bad and I didn't feel good. I felt nothing. I certainly didn't congratulate myself but I didn't judge myself either. It was just a very neutral feeling, almost like indifference.

Then I went clothes shopping, which was something else I used to do. And once again I felt nothing. I really started to worry, because all of my go-to stuff seemed to be *done*.

What did this mean? I started to realize the real essence of my addiction. My attachments to drugs, alcohol, and sex, and to being a big shot, were only *secondary* addictions.

My real addiction was to the *drama* that those things created. When that drama was

WHEN THAT DRAMA WAS GONE, WHEN THERE WASN'T INTENSITY ANYMORE— EVEN IF THE INTENSITY WAS SELF-CONDEMNATION— I FELT LIKE I WAS DRIFTING IN THE MIDDLE OF THE OCEAN.

gone, when there wasn't intensity anymore—even if the intensity was self-condemnation—I felt like I was drifting in the middle of the ocean.

That lack of drama is going to affect you when you reconnect with your wholeness. It's a huge transition, and despite the fact that reconnecting with your soul self is very positive, there will be a time when you experience it as depression. It's an adjustment period and it happens to almost everybody. You need to adjust to the absence of what was always there in your life. Even though it was terrible, it was what you were used to. When you experience the splitting away from your wholeness, you filled the empty space with drama. That drama was a way of preventing you from seeing what had really happened. It was like a whole stage full of scenery that was so colorful and compelling that you couldn't see what the stage really looked like. It was like watching an actor play a part so well that you never gave much thought to who the real person was like.

Meanwhile, we're still aware deep down that there's something beyond the drama. There's something more important than all the distraction we've placed between who we are right now and our true wholeness. That's why we chase after anything that seems to offer a spiritual connection. We're desperate for that connection, so we'll try any healer, any chant, any meditation, or whatever seems most popular in the moment. Many people will also try any substance, whether it's alcohol or opioids or you name it. Then when you finally get what you've been looking for, you've suddenly got a lot more peace and even a lot more time than you've been used to. Among other things, dealing with stress in your career or stress in relationships takes a lot of time, and suddenly all those things are going really well. How do you handle *that*?

ADJUSTING TO THE NEW NORMAL

You'll start to feel better when you really accept the fact that the change you feel is a permanent condition. It can't be taken away. The depression you felt shortly after the change happened was at least partly because you were afraid the change might somehow reverse itself. But as a little time goes by you'll see how that's not going to happen. You thought you needed excitement. You had become dependent on a high level of external stimulation. But you'll begin to like peacefulness. It's a new experience so it takes some getting used to, but you'll begin to like it.

Then you'll see how what you had before was a strategy for distracting yourself.

Again, this adjustment period happens to everyone. For some people it's days, for others it takes a few weeks. But there are some things that can make it easier.

- **A daily spiritual practice.** This can include meditation, yoga, prayer, or even running. It's anything that directs your consciousness above and away from the stresses of everyday life. But to meet the definition of daily practice, you need to do it every day. That should seem obvious, but a majority of people don't get it. When I ask them why, they usually give one of two reasons. Either things are going well, so there's no need for a spiritual practice, or things are going badly, so what's the use because it doesn't work? My recommendation, however, is that you do your spiritual practice for at least fourteen days after your reconnection, regardless of how you're feeling. And if you don't already have a spiritual practice, investigate what seems comfortable for you and get started.

- **Nutritious food.** It isn't so much that you need to be improving your health every time you have lunch or dinner. It isn't that you have to be getting better all the time. But if you're starting to feel stressed or anxious, unhealthy food can amplify those feelings. It can make the situation worse. That's why we suggest staying away from processed foods and emphasizing fruits and vegetables to the degree that you feel comfortable.

- **See who you were "before."** Find a photo of yourself when you were very young, before the splitting off from your soul took place. As you look at that photograph, be aware that this is the person with whom you've made a new and permanent agreement. This is the person who is now making the decisions in your life. You'll reach a point where you close your eyes and ask the person in the picture about making a decision, and you'll see that person nod yes or no, and you'll know what to do. Keep that picture in mind, and put it on your cell phone. Look at it every day when you're ready to do your spiritual practice.

As you take these positive steps, I want you also to get beyond some feelings that are nothing but misunderstandings. For instance, if you reconnected with your soul in Costa Rica, or at a certain time of year, you may also want to be in the presence of the 'people who were with you when you made the connection. You may even feel you need to be with those people because, after all, they were there at one of the most important moments of your life. For practical reasons, that kind of reunion isn't always possible. It may be very difficult to put together. But I genuinely believe that at some higher level of being you are present with those people who are so important to you. You can always connect with them as part of your spiritual practice, and when the opportunity is right, you'll be able to meet with them again in person.

The important thing to remember is that you have everything you need, and you will always have it from now on. As we've said, it's natural to fear that you'll lose what you've gained, or that it might somehow be taken away from you. But that isn't going to happen.

Once you really embrace the permanent nature of the change you've made, you'll also begin to see the responsibility and opportunity that comes with that change.

YOU'VE GOT WORK TO DO

There's important work for you to do in the world based on the capabilities of the new wholeness you've achieved. That work can take many forms. Stay open to the possibilities and you'll recognize the right ones as they begin to appear. Be aware of the fact that you can get used to anything, and that you want to keep your new energy strong. I was born in Scranton, Pennsylvania, which is not one of the most picturesque locations in America. Much later, when I moved to Malibu, California, for the first two years I couldn't get over how beautiful it was.

I was lucky I didn't get in an accident, because I would drive down the Pacific Coast Highway and I couldn't take my eyes off the ocean. I don't think I ever looked at the road. That huge vision of the bright blue water was just too overwhelming.

But then what happened? After a couple of years, I got used to it. I took it for granted. I was on the same highway and the view was the same, but I was just looking at the traffic like everybody else. Habits are easy to develop and they're hard to break, even when you've experienced a profound transformation. You've been living outside yourself for a very long time, in the sense that how you feel and what you do has been governed by external events. Now you're living within yourself, but some of those habits are still there. You might still feel the habit of behaving in a certain way. But compared to how you felt in the past, you'll also feel differently when you do that.

A few weeks after I found my soul, I was driving down the street and somebody cut me off in traffic. Over the years when something like that happened, I had developed a habitual response. I would get even. I was going to take out my anger on whoever had disrespected me. I had been injured, which felt bad, and I was going to injure somebody in return, which always felt great. That was the habit I'd developed. Not long after I got back from my first trip to Costa Rica, I was driving in Los Angeles when somebody cut me off in traffic. The old habit kicked in. I had a plastic water bottle with me, so I caught up to the woman and threw the bottle at her car. It was the old force of habit. But it didn't give me the jolt of energy I used to feel. It didn't give me anything except a feeling of emptiness.

Over time I started to recognize that feeling of emptiness that would happen whenever I reverted to my past behavior. I didn't really feel critical of myself, and I certainly didn't feel proud of myself. I just felt like I was neutrally watching myself doing something that made no sense, and was out of sync with the person I really am.

Finding the right work in the world is the best way to keep the new energy of your connection alive. By sharing what you're feeling right now, you'll be able to keep feeling it at full force. And when you begin to see people around you making their own connections, yours will grow even stronger.

Chapter Seven

RYTHMIA

LIFECHANGING!
Rythmia saved my life!
I connected with my higher power
and inner child through the magic of
plant medicine. The staff were all
SO NICE and accommodating.
I felt like I was at home away from home.
I am seriously so blessed to have had
such an incredible opportunity just fall
into my lap like this did. I used to wake up
miserable every day, but now I wake up
and I look at life through a child's eyes;
I'm curious about what life has to offer,
and I love confidently with no fear.

—A Rythmia guest

The days immediately after my first plant
medicine journey felt like the first days of a new life.
I felt completely changed, different to the core. I didn't

want to smoke, I didn't want to drink. I noticed when I said "hello" to somebody, I really *meant* hello. When I said, "How are you?" I genuinely wanted to know how that person was feeling. I didn't mean, "I couldn't care less about how you're feeling and I'm just trying to get rid of you."

What have I learned? It's hard to put it into a few words. I learned that only love really exists, but what does that really mean? I could say that I can't hurt another person without hurting myself. Or that I always will be helping myself whenever I help someone else. I'm not just saying these things. I've actually seen them and felt them. Almost from the beginning, I felt I was embarking on a mission to create a place in Costa Rica where other people could discover what I had learned. I decided to call it Rythmia.

It was around that time that another life-changing event happened. I met Brandee, the love of my life, my partner in my life's work, and now my wife. It was divine order. I met her because I was ready to meet her, and I was ready because of what I had learned from the moon.

In my first marriage, I was not ready. I was really bad to my first wife and I want to be honest about that here. I first met her in 1980. We were married in 1990 and had two amazing children. The marriage lasted until 2012, so in total we were together more or less for thirty-two years.

My heart breaks for her every time I think of her, and I think of her often. She was born to a family with a history of abuse of all kinds, and a mom who was simply out of touch. For my wife, this experience produced a woman with an attachment disorder similar to my own. Basically, that meant an inability to trust. I may have been slightly more aware of things than she was, but I was also much angrier. I couldn't get close, I didn't understand why, and I was pissed off about it. My wife saw things more simply and just glossed over our lack of connection. I was terrible to her. I literally hated her for how she was, without at all considering the effects of the environment she'd come from. I am forever regretful of how I treated her. Despite her attachment issues, she was a great mother and what she lacked in affection for the kids she made up for by always being there and being a truly responsible person. To this day, I love her and always will. I have so much regret from that time in my life.

In the past, I couldn't have a relationship with anyone. I was unable to be present, I was untrustworthy and had trouble really feeling anything. I knew something was wrong with me and I didn't know what it was. But shortly after my first experience in Costa Rica, I met this woman who I was crazy about. I could hardly believe that I could be with someone who was so open and loving, and who even shared the same passions and goals that I feel. Brandee has been with me at every step of Rythmia's evolution. We are truly in it together.

I continue to be amazed by the grace that can be redeemed by reunification with one's soul, and also through unification with a true soulmate. The medicine has shown me that every single minute is a gift and that nothing is certain. The medicine has also shown me that anything is possible, and my life with Brandee is living proof of that.

Because of my past, I just didn't think that could happen. And here's the biggest miracle: I realized that I could love someone—and I could even be loved in return.

Now, at a different time in my life, I'm filled with hope and love and I'm ready to create a fulfilling partnership in my new marriage. When we met, Brandee had recently had a plant medicine experience that was similar to mine. When she asked the medicine about her life's purpose, her entire consciousness suddenly changed. She saw her past differently, and her she saw her future even more differently.

Brandee's father had taken his own life when she was only six years old. From then on, she became the nurturer and protector of her surviving parent: the "mother of her mother."

The plant showed Brandee how her whole experience of playing the role of nurturing mother had prepared her for a hugely expanded nurturing role. Brandee's true purpose would be to nurture an enterprise that could literally transform the planet. From that moment, she could see a well-lit path before her. She resigned from her other marketing agency clients to focus all her energy on the vision that had been revealed to her—and to us—and continues to play a critical role in helping me evolve the guest experiences at Rythmia.

Our vision for Rythmia was, and still is, to help visitors accomplish three important life tasks:

First, to recognize who they are right now. That is, who they have become over the years, as a step toward reconnecting and merging back with their soul.

Second, as that reconnection takes place, to heal their hearts.

Third, with their hearts healed, to meet the rest of their soul family. These are the people with whom you feel a deep connection—not your birth family, but those with like souls, emotions, and beliefs. Some may feel the connection goes back through many lifetimes. They can be people you meet at the center, or people in your everyday life (e.g., your yoga teacher or a spiritual leader). Together, you begin to heal the world.

If that third step seems like an ambitious enterprise, I've seen that what happens at Rythmia naturally extends beyond individual lives. I know that people who come to Rythmia will go on to help other people make their own changes. The moon taught me to think of these people in two categories: Light Workers and Light Warriors. Lately, the moon has described that Light Workers are our feminine side and Light Warriors are our masculine side. Each of us has both. Being both a Light Worker and a Light Warrior is a big job, but we have been given a very big job of transforming the world together. I know that this sounds crazy, but the moon said that this is exactly what was going to happen.

Rythmia would be a spiritual resort, and also a medically licensed venue for issues of addiction and general health. I decided to call it a life advancement center, a place where people could take their lives to a new level in an impeccably welcoming, supportive, and safe environment. Visitors would take part in a program designed to merge them back with their souls in just seven nights.

When I experienced my first plant medicine ceremony in Costa Rica, I was shocked by the conditions at that facility. It was dirty, the food wasn't good, and I honestly didn't trust anybody. But I was already committed; I had already paid for my stay. I'm grateful for what happened there, but the location was completely out of sync with the intense emotional and spiritual experience I had. Suppose I were to ask someone, "Would you go to Peru, hike up a trail, ride a donkey, and spend a rainy night in a tent if it would make you healthier?" Some people would go for that, but most would decline.

I thought, *What if this could be done in an ideal setting? A place with the vibe of a high-end retreat?* I knew that a significant number of people would be interested in a life-advancement opportunity if it took place in an environment that was comfortable and reassuring. There would be farm-to-table organic food, a luxurious spa, beautiful rooms, and all the things that were missing from my first experience. Definitely a pool. There would be a medical certification and a medical staff to put people at ease.

When visitors leave Rythmia, more than 90 percent say they had a life-changing miracle during their week-long stay. They report this on their e-mail surveys after they depart.

Why does this positive experience happen so consistently? It's because we know the importance of having guides from authentic spiritual traditions. We know the benefits of an amazing natural environment combined with first-rate medical support. Approximately half of Rythmia's visitors choose to participate in the plant medicine ceremonies and the other half in Rythmic Breath Work, or both. Many are having this kind of experience for the first time, while others have had a prior experience. In both cases, guests report that the first time they had a genuinely meaningful result was when they came to Rythmia. Despite what people might assume, there really isn't a deep distinction between plant medicine and other forms of spiritual experience such as breath work or yoga. At Rythmia, they all lead to merging back with your soul.

As with any intervention on long-established habits and lifestyles—even obviously destructive ones—there can be resistance to change at first. But one of the most gratifying parts of my work at Rythmia is seeing how quickly and deeply positive change can happen.

Many Rythmia visitors are highly educated, very successful people. Quite understandably, they may think they're smarter than everybody else, and often they're right about that. There are times when even plant medicine can reinforce that sense of superiority. The medicine can show you things in greater depth, so now you think you're really smarter than everybody else.

If you ask ego-based questions like, "Can you show me what a great guy I am?" you may get the answer you want. But in the right setting, with the right guidance and the right intention, a permanent and positive life-changing experience can happen, and it can happen in just one week.

Many people say they want to bring help to the world. They say they want to do this or that, and they mean well. But the first and the best thing you have to do is to get back to your whole selves. Only then you find what's right for you, not because you've made a program for yourself, but because it's right for you. One of the things I've learned by doing plant medicine and breath work is the concept of collective accountability. Yes, each of us has our own journey and we're responsible for what we did, and also how we responded to what other people did. That kind of responsibility can be challenging, but the alternative is to see ourselves as victims, which is not a good direction at all.

Beyond individual accountability, *collective* accountability means taking positive action for what humanity as a whole has done, and for what has been done to humanity. That action can be on a large philanthropic scale, for people who have the resources, or it can be on a more modest scale. But it shouldn't be guys sitting around the country club bragging about their charities. That's not real, and the medicine shows you what's real and what isn't.

I believe that the sooner you see what's real, the better off you'll be—and the more you'll be able to accomplish. I've seen a lot of kids right out of college or with a new MBA. They're totally motivated, but for what? They want to cash big checks. I understand that. You can't just tell young people that they're materialistic, or that they're superficial. But if that motivation could be channeled in a more humanistic direction, there would be great possibilities for everybody. Creating those channels is the shared basis of everything we do at Rythmia, with the channels existing in a variety of forms. For example:

> Yoga has become such a hugely popular activity in the United States that it could honestly be called a revolution. In simplest terms, yoga is a discipline that enhances physical health and spiritual development through combined use of exercise and meditative practice. In a larger sense, yoga can be a tool for profound transformation. Toward that goal, at Rythmia we have mindfully created a yoga temple to support

the practice. Students on all levels, beginner to expert, are welcomed to participate, daily, and are empowered to experience *prana*—the universal source of breath, life energy, and conscious intelligence—as the navigating source of yoga practice and vital living.

Dead Sea Cleanse is a complete hydrotherapy treatment designed to rid your body of any parasites and toxins. For genuine well-being, it's essential for your physical body to be a clean and healed vessel in which your spiritual self can reside. Research has shown that having microorganisms inhabiting the body can have an impact on how we feel and act. Based on consultation with Rythmia's cleanse specialist, a plan is developed commensurate with the length of stay at Rythmia.

In Part Two you'll find some breath-of-life exercises that you can try right away.

And last but not least, there's "Sh*t the Moon Said"—in her own words!

THE MIRACLE, THE MOON, AND YOU

Chapter Eight

BREATH OF LIFE

When I talked with the moon, I was the one who usually asked the questions. But in one of our most important conversations, the moon asked some questions of me.

I was trying to learn as much as I could about the process of merging with my soul. I tried to think of it as a roadmap. Was there only one way to reach the destination, or were there many ways? I asked the moon about this, and that was when she replied to my question with a question of her own. It was one that really caught me off guard.

The moon said, "Have you ever seen anyone die?"

"Yes," I said, "I saw my father die."

"What exactly did you see?"

Of course, I had a very clear memory of my father's death. It seemed mysterious to me, it seemed to be fulfilling for him. He was obviously seeing some things that were invisible to everyone but him.

"It was like he was talking to people from his past," I said, "even from his early childhood. It seemed to be more than just talking with those people. It was like he was really together with them in some place I couldn't see."

"This can be the answer to your question," the moon said. "In the very last moments of his life, your father arrived at the destination you want to reach. He merged with his soul self. The truth is, everyone arrives at that destination sooner or later, even if it's in the last moments of life. All roads lead to that experience. But no one needs to wait until the end of life to get there. There are some shortcuts you can take long before your death."

"That's what I want to learn about," I said. "How else can I get there?"

What the moon said next was truly life-changing information. She told me there were two broad pathways to merging with your soul. One was through plant medicine, which I had already discovered. The other—as in yoga and other spiritual traditions—was through breath control as a gateway to meditation and visionary experience.

This was a huge revelation for me. The fact that merging with the soul could happen without plant medicine opened huge opportunities for sharing the moon's wisdom with an unlimited number of people. This lead to the creation of Rythmic Breath Work, a program of breathing exercises and vision work that achieves the same results as plant medicine.

Our Rythmic Breath Work is a program based on the incredibly powerful mechanism that is the human breath. For centuries many cultures, especially in the East, have recognized that power. But in everyday American life, most people breathe using only 20 percent of their respiratory potential and aren't even aware why this is important. As a rule, we don't give our breathing a second thought. We know why we're breathing—to stay alive—but we pay no attention to how it's happening. We may take quick short breaths all day long, then lie down at night and take the first (and also the last) deep breath of the past twenty-four hours. Anyone who brought that same approach to other vital functions, such as eating or drinking, definitely would not last very long.

The first step for using the Rythmic Breath Work for merging back with your soul is to take a quick look at who you are right now. The questions below will help you do that. They're not intended to provide you with a full-scale self-analysis, but they can give you an idea about whether your self-image is primarily positive or negative. This will help you arrive at the best starting point for the breath work that follows.

As you answer these questions, don't feel that you need to spend much time on them. Try to be spontaneous and, of course, be honest. Just answer yes or no to each question.

Are you a trustworthy person?
Do you generally finish tasks you start?
Are you a friendly person?
Do you have a good sense of humor?
Are you generally an energetic person?
Are you able to admit your mistakes?
Are you assertive when you need to be?
Do you stay calm in tense situations?
Are you helpful to others?

If you answered yes to all or nearly all of the questions, you're ready to get started with Rythmic Breath Work. Your sense of yourself is appropriately positive. If your response was mostly negative, be open to the possibility that you're judging yourself too harshly. Then even if you don't feel you deserve it, take a moment to completely forgive yourself, at least for the duration of the breath work that follows. Forgiving yourself—and forgiving other people, too—is a big part of any spiritual work, and it's essential for the Rythmic Breath Work exercise we're going to begin now.

Let me repeat what the moon told me. There are many ways to merge back with your soul. Plant medicine is one way. Meditation is another way, and breath work is an especially accessible and effective connecting point for meditation. Rythmic Breath Work exercises have three interlocking benefits:

First, the exercises help you physically. Rythmic Breathing opens your respiratory system so that you can use its full capacity.

Second, Rythmic Breathing helps clear negativity that physically manifests in your respiration.

Third, and perhaps most important, there are spiritual benefits from enhanced breathing. Clearing away physical and emotional obstacles opens a path for soul connection.

When you're ready to begin, find a place where you won't be interrupted for a while. Wear comfortable clothing and take a moment to separate your thoughts from everyday concerns. Feel your body settling into a tranquil state as you prepare for the session.

The Rythmic Breath Work has three steps:

First, bring focused concentration to inhaling each breath, so that you can inhale deeply.

Second, relax completely as you exhale.

Third, while continuing to inhale and exhale deeply and comfortably, close your eyes and bring focused attention to the following three visual images. Spend a few minutes creating the images in your mind's eye, and then take at least five minutes visualizing the images, one after the other. You'll probably want to open your eyes for a minute or two before progressing from one image to the next.

STEP 1:
SHOW ME WHO I'VE BECOME

The first image should express who you are now—who is this person that you've become over the course of your life? Imagine some snapshots of yourself in different kinds of settings, some relaxed and comfortable, and others more challenging. What does the expression on your face look like in those situations? How do you feel in your heart when you see them? Try to be completely honest with yourself because, after all, you're the only one who's ever going to see these imaginary photos, so try to make the most of them.

After you've taken a short break, you can begin the second visualization.

STEP 2.
MERGE ME BACK WITH MY SOUL

With your eyes closed, try to picture your very earliest memories. This should include not just what the location looked like, but any other sensory elements you can manage to remember. What were the sounds and smells? Do you remember touching anything? What was the texture? Was it hot or cold?

Ideally, this becomes more than just a memory. It should almost turn into a kind of time travel, especially when you make your very young self a part of the image. Feel the person you are now merging with that small child—and be aware that the child is who you were before any sort of trauma separated you from that very young human being.

You'll want to put some real energy into making this second visualization as authentic as possible. With practice, it can become a deeply emotional experience, or even a miraculous one. But even though this can seem like the most powerful of the Rythmic Breath Work visualizations, it's important to do all three of them in sequence. Somehow they're both separate and not separate at the same time. That's part of the mystery of the Rythmic Breath Work, and also part of its power.

STEP 3:
HEAL MY HEART

The last of the three visualizations might be the most imaginative, because you'll be picturing a person you've never actually seen. In fact, you'll picture a being that isn't even a person at all. Instead, using whatever ideation seems most comfortable and inspiring to you, imagine a supremely wise and compassionate presence—yes, let's call that God— healing your heart at the deepest level. Feel the conflicts and contradictions of your life instantly and completely resolving—especially those that began with your traumatic separation from your soul identity. It's a wonderful feeling when that happens, and you can make it happen with this visualization.

Finish by sitting quietly for a few moments with your eyes closed. Breathe slowly and deeply. Then open your eyes and return to the world. The world may not have changed, but you certainly have.

Chapter Nine

SH*T THE MOON SAID

Within a short time after I bought the property in Costa Rica, the moon gave me something even more amazing than beautiful Rythmia. She gave me a basic explanation of how our lives really work, and what we have to do in order to lead fulfilling lives. We're all born with our souls intact. We only want four things:

1. We want to love.
2. We want to be loved.
3. We want a sense of community; a feeling of belonging.

4. We want the experience of joy.

We want to have fun. We want to have as much fun as possible. I had fun in my dialogue with the moon, and some of my questions are more irreverent than you might expect. Others are rather deep, or at least that's what I intended. I hope these questions and answers give you much to think about, and I hope they inspire some questions of your own. That way, you and the moon will have lots to talk about.

A CONVERSATION WITH THE MOON

How can I be happy and live at peace?

Be the truth. Live an authentic life.

It was time to shed the stories, time to stop telling half-truths and white lies. It was time to be honorable. It was time to get real so that my intentions and actions were aligned. It sounded scary, but deep down inside I just wanted to find who I really was so I could be an authentic me.

How should I do that?

Stop shining light on things that aren't really you.

I had a deep desire to show others how I could defy their logic and their limits. By doing that, I could be the center of attention, appreciated, and loved by everyone. This led to my insecurity and my fears of not being "enough." I was trying to be everything to everyone.

Why am I here?

Life is a gift for you to open and enjoy.
It's that simple.

I needed to stop excessive analyzing and complicating every aspect of my existence. The time had come to discover the meaning of authentic happiness and point my life in that direction.

On what should I be spending my time?

There's no time for drama. There's always time for love and new experience.

It was time to shift my focus toward love: love for self, which is not the same as egotism; love for family. Creating relationships where love can be authentically shared. Whatever we focus on expands. That needs to be the goal, while also eliminating situations and relationships that bring toxic, time-wasting drama to my life.

Does life have a beginning and an end?

You were never born and you will never die.

Our existence is not limited to our physical selves. We are all spirits. Our spirit has been present before this existence, and will continue on into infinity. Recognizing union with the immortal spirit is challenging but reassuring, and most of all, it's inspiring.

Where are the records of my life stored?

They are stored in your soul, not in your mind.

The soul is the keeper of everyone's story. The mind has no role to play in the discovery, or the history, or the meaning of our existence.

Where is heaven?

Heaven and hell are in the same place within you.

I have the power to choose love or fear, good or bad, trust or judgment. I own the decision to choose the emotion and the intention that will yield one outcome or another: heaven or hell.

Is being happy more difficult when you're smart?

Knowledge gains no points from the universe. Authenticity and love gain all the points.

All the brains (and money!) in the world will get you nowhere fast. The universe honors, respects, and rewards those whose sole (soul!) intent is to be a selfless hero.

How can I have a good life?

Choose only what's good for your "Eternal Child"—that is, for your soul.

Our souls are like children. Innocent, curious, full of love and trust. But we lose our soul connection very early in life—by five or six years old—owing to trauma or to another event that says, "It's no longer safe to be you." This is when we disconnect from our soul. Now, when making decisions, I've learned to ask myself, What would I choose for the child version of me?

Is there such a thing as bad luck?

No, you manifest everything:
good and bad, ugly and beautiful, and
whatever else is in between.

Our thoughts and words are powerful tools. Through them, we choose our destiny. So choose your thoughts and words purposefully and with positive intent for the good of yourself and for those affected by you.

What urgent advice can you give me?

Use your time wisely.

Time is of the essence. Invest time in what brings you bountiful joy and pure love. Everything else is a waste of time.

What should I do if I get stuck in regret?

Know that the past does not exist.
Only this moment and the future are real.

The past is just that. It already happened. Looking in the rearview mirror won't allow you to live fully in the present moment, or prepare you for your future. Fixating on where you've been prevents you from getting where you want to go.

Why don't I know what I want?

When you know exactly what you want, that's when you will know exactly what you want.

Getting clear on what you want is a process. It starts with understanding who you are and who you are not. Only then can you determine your deepest desires. It's important to not be distracted by the desires of those you are trying to please. This is your life, your dream, your present, and your future.

How can I learn to see you?

Meditate in order to know me, to see God,
and to find yourself.

Be still and you can find God. God is within you. God is within every living thing, in every cell. Be still and God will appear to you.

Am I supposed to be monogamous?

To be really happy, you should be with just
one person. But do whatever you want
as long as you're honest with everyone
concerned.

Being open, honest, and truthful to yourself and those around you is the Golden Rule for all relationships. It is up to you to define your happiness. If monogamy is what you desire, then share this with your partner. If this is not your desire, then find like-minded people.

How can I repent?

Be truthful, and never hurt another person
intentionally.

Everyone makes mistakes, but a spiritually advanced person stops repeating them. Learn from your mistakes and take responsibility for them. Then you can move forward with a clear conscience.

How can I stop texting women?

Texting requires moving your fingers.
Doing nothing requires nothing.
Doing nothing is easier!

Sometimes it's easiest and best to surrender and do nothing. It's effortless. When we force energy and create friction in unrewarding directions, it can only ricochet back at us.

When I feel weak, how can I feel stronger?

See strength in your weakness and resilience in your vulnerability.

Go directly to the source of what is making you feel weak. Acknowledge the weakness. Invite the weakness in. Embrace the weakness. In this way you demonstrate—even to the weakness itself—that you are strong and are now in control.

If I create this setting in which plant medicine ceremonies could take place, what is going to happen to the world?

As more people take part in the ceremonies, more people will see themselves for who they really are. The more people who act upon this truth, the better it will be for all.

Plant medicine ceremonies can help many people find their inner truth. They can gain power to fulfill the potential of their lives, and this would benefit everyone. Once this is understood, there is a social responsibility to invite as many people as possible to the ceremonies.

How should I deal with temptation?

Choose honor instead of convenient escape.

This is a theme the moon keeps repeating: I have a choice to make between my heaven and my hell. For much of my life I had been choosing the quick fix, the "life hack" to numb my reality. This may always be a temptation, but one I need to resist.

When I forget what I've learned and start looking outside myself, how can I stop?

Remember that nothing is really outside yourself. Whatever you're seeking is inside yourself, including God.

Because we are one with Spirit, or God, we have access at all times. My true authentic self is within me. With awareness of this unity we are able to live a life filled with love.

To whom should I pray?

You are the God of you. Pray to your higher self or anyone you choose, as God is everything and everything is God.

It's our nature to question, and all the answers are within ourselves.

What religion should I follow?

Live without anyone's religion. Listen to nature. Don't rely on anyone's experience except your own. You have your own religion, just as everyone does.

"I am the master of my fate: I am the captain of my soul," from "Invictus," a poem by William Ernest Henley, published in 1888.

Do I need to meditate?

Yes, so you can visit me.

In the stillness of meditation, you can find a sense of self. No matter what your question might be, the answers are within.

How can disease be healed?

Reconnect the soul with the body.

Feed the body vegetables, "nature's little miracles," and the body will heal itself. Once we are able to embrace the trauma of childhood—the moment disconnection from our soul took place—we can reconnect to our authentic selves. Once this occurs, we are responsible for nurturing ourselves through nature's food.

What should I do if someone hurts me so badly that I can't forgive them?

When your soul is back in your body, you will find that forgiveness is easy.

The part of you that was hurt was a false part of you. The part of you that forgives, your soul, can never be harmed or endangered. Your soul owns the wholeness of you. It is not a thing or a thought or an emotion that can be affected by exterior forces.

Why do we need to disconnect and forget our true selves? Why do we need to become someone else?

You were designed to forget, which is the only way to expand your consciousness. You need to feel completely new and alone in order to understand that you're not alone at all.

People are like technology. We arrive with a full operating system including hardware and software. Then we are programmed, reprogrammed, stuff comes in/stuff goes out, and we are left with a compromised system. Until we debug the system and press the "refresh" button, we aren't able to clear and trust the operating system we came in with.

How can I remove darkness from my life?

You can't remove it. If you are afraid of it or try to avoid it, you will have a lifelong losing battle. Just love the darkness and it will lose all power over you.

We have to sit in darkness sometimes and acknowledge its presence, and acknowledge it does not have power over us. Embrace the darkness and trust tomorrow is a bright new day filled with limitless possibilities.

Sometimes it all seems so hard. Can you do me a big favor? In my next life, could you bring me to my soul connection very quickly? Can I find happiness right away?

Gerry, that's a request about next time, but it's the same request you used last time.

If this last question and answer sounds familiar, that's because they're basically the same ones that opened this book. How can we find happiness in the true sense of the word, and how can we find it sooner rather than later? There is a simple answer to this, but it's not necessarily an easy one. As I've tried to show in these pages, happiness becomes possible when connection with our souls is restored. This is the wisdom of the *Bhagavad Gita*, one of the world's great spiritual texts, which teaches that our soul is waiting in infinity for us to discover it again. That discovery, that reconnection, can happen in many ways, and it can happen at any time: today, or this week, or this month, or perhaps "next time," as the moon said, when the universe recycles us back into this existence again. But you will reconnect with your soul, I'm sure of that. And if this book helps you to do it quickly, then I will certainly feel happiness. More than that, I will feel truly blessed.

ABOUT THE AUTHOR

Gerard Armond Powell is a conscious entrepreneur, thought leader, philanthropist, and public speaker whose mission is to transform lives.

He is the founder of Rythmia Life Advancement Center in Costa Rica, the "go-to" facility for a spiritually awakening vacation experience that combines first-class amenities, organic farm-to-table meals, and world-renowned specialists —all under one roof. Some of the transformational modalities offered at Rythmia are:

"The Answer is You" Workshop created by Michael Beckwith
The Dead Sea Cleanse: a hydrotherapy colonic cleanse
Yoga
Plant Medicine
Rythmic Breath Work

Gerard has also founded *Truthenomics*, an online program teaching the skills and insights essential to living a life of manifestation.

His early business ventures were nothing short of miraculous. In 1991, while still in his twenties, Gerard's partnership with a building and development company resulted in a consummate deal netting him more than a million dollars.

Gerard went on to build multiple companies, such as *thatlook.com*, the first company organized to provide mass-market access to cosmetic surgery procedures. It went public in 1999 and achieved a market value of approximately $150 million. Gerard and his management team subsequently founded *My Choice Medical Inc.*, which he sold for over $89,000,000 in 2004, and then quit working.

Despite achieving "the American dream," Gerard knew that something was missing. The more he achieved, the more he fell into depression. Through a personal crisis, struggling with alcoholism and thoughts of suicide, he was initiated into a journey of self-transformation. He traveled the world and spent hundreds of thousands of dollars in search of every healing modality he could find.

One night, through a powerful encounter with plant medicine, Gerard's existence was transformed and he was liberated from a lifetime of suffering.

After this life-altering experience, Gerard was inspired to create Rythmia, a place that could offer—at an affordable price and to as many people as possible—the very same healing modalities that engendered his own transformation.

Rythmia and Gerard's story are featured in a newly released documentary, "The Reality of Truth," which includes conversations with thought leaders such as Joel Osteen, Sri Sri Ravi Shankar, Deepak Chopra, Marianne Williamson, and more, as well Hollywood stars Michelle Rodriguez and Peter Coyote.

Gerard is a leader in a growing conscious business movement that recognizes the profound importance of personal healing and spiritual transformation as integral parts of our lives. As a conscious entrepreneur who speaks to audiences and organizations, Gerry is known for his unfiltered style, his humor and authenticity, and his ability to inspire.

For additional information about Gerard Armond Powell, or for speaking inquiries, please email *haamid@rythmia.com* or visit *gerardarmondpowell.com*.

If you're interested in joining Gerard and his mission, or would like to learn more, check out:

www.rythmia.com

www.gerardarmondpowell.com

Follow Gerard and his team on social media:

www.facebook.com/rythmia
www.facebook.com/gerardarmondpowell
www.facebook.com/sh*tthemoonsaid

www.instagram.com/rythmia_
www.instagram.com/gerardarmondpowell
www.instagram.com/sh*tthemoonsaid

www.youtube.com/rythmialifeadvancementcenter
www.youtube.com/gerardarmondpowell